W9-AEZ-923

Fn. Schmeder

# SEARCHING THE SCRIPTURES

# SEARCHING THE SCRIPTURES

## JOHN J. DOUGHERTY

*Professor of Sacred Scripture*

## HANOVER HOUSE

*A Division of Doubleday & Company, Inc.*

*Garden City, New York*

Nihil Obstat: Peter B. O'Connor, P.A., LL.D.
             Censor Librorum

Imprimatur: ✠ Thomas A. Boland, S.T.D.
             Archbishop of Newark
             August 18, 1959

Old Testament quotations are from the Douay Version,
the Confraternity Edition, *The Complete Bible* of the
University of Chicago (a non-Catholic version), and
*The Book of Isaiah* by Msgr. E. J. Kissane. New Testament quotations are from the Confraternity Edition and
the New Testament translation of Fr. F. A. Spencer, O.P.

Library of Congress Catalog Card Number 59–12624
Copyright © 1959 by Doubleday & Company, Inc.
All Rights Reserved
Printed in the United States of America

TO

*Mary and Christine*

# PREFACE

This book is addressed to those who desire to engage in serious Bible reading, but who are laymen in biblical science. It is mostly a matter of orientation and illustration, a sort of bridge between the common reader and the world of biblical scholarship. Contemporary research has rendered distinguished service to the Bible. It seems fitting that the layman should share in the fruits of that research so that he may come to a fuller understanding of the Word of God.

Recent advances in biblical scholarship are in the areas of criticism and interpretation. Although at the moment much is conjectural and tentative, definite gains have been made, and we are moving in the right direction. This book is an attempt to bring to the layman in a popular way some of these gains and to point out the reasons for the new directions in interpretation, particularly among Catholic scholars.

The experience of most Catholics with the Bible is one of hearing rather than of reading. They hear it read in the churches at Sunday Masses. This is a very limited experience in the Bible since they hear only brief excerpts from the New Testament. It is, however, for the great cross section of Catholics, a contact with the Word of God in the living experience of worship. Those enjoy a fuller experience of the Scriptures who read the English Missal and attend Mass more frequently. This is true of so many who attend Mass daily during the Lenten season. The Masses of Lent combine texts from the Old and New Testaments in a liturgical fabric that is truly inspired art. The appreciation of this can be increased by a thoughtful reading of Pius Parsch's *The Church's Year of Grace*.

The intimate bond between the liturgy and the Bible has proved a rich field of research for contemporary biblical scholars and liturgists. Worthy of special mention in this regard are the studies published by the Liturgical Committee of the University of Notre Dame, such works as Fr. Jean Daniélou's *The Bible and the Liturgy* and Fr. Louis Bouyer's *The Meaning of Sacred Scripture*. The distinguished liturgical quarterly *Worship* published by the Benedictines of St. John's Abbey, Collegeville, Minnesota provides stimulating articles on the Bible as well as the liturgy.

The Bible reaches every Catholic in some measure through the public worship of the Church. In addition to the Mass there is the Divine Office, which is read by priests and religious, and by a devout laity. The Breviary is made up for the most part of Psalms and Scripture readings. There is a weekly cycle of readings from the Psalter and an annual cycle of readings from the rest of the Bible, beginning on Septuagesima Sunday. It will appear from these observations that the Bible is in a real sense part of the Church's very life. If the sacraments are the daily nourishment of the Church, the Bible is the air it daily breathes.

At this point one might ask, "Is there any need then for private Bible reading?" The question may be understood in two ways. If it means "Is Bible reading necessary for salvation?" the answer is no. If it means "Is Bible reading spiritually profitable?" the answer is a resounding yes, and that on no less an authority than St. Paul. The Apostle assures us that the Scriptures "are able to instruct us unto salvation by the faith which is in Christ Jesus" (2 Tim. 3:15). The late Holy Father, Pope Pius XII, in his encyclical *Divino Afflante Spiritu* quoted these words of St. Jerome: "If there is anything in this life which sustains a wise man and induces him to maintain his serenity amidst the tribulations and adversities of the world, it is in the first place, I consider, the meditation and knowledge of the Scriptures." No more concrete expression of the Church's encouragement of private reading of the Scriptures could be asked than the fact that she confers the spiritual benefits of indulgences on her children who read the Bible. Pope Leo XIII ordained that "the faithful who spend at least a quarter of an hour in reading Holy Scripture with the great reverence due to the Word of God and after the manner of spiritual reading may gain an Indulgence of 300 days."

A plenary indulgence may be gained once a month by those who make private reading a daily practice.

In light of these realities it is hard to see how any vestige of the impression could survive that the Catholic Church is opposed to private Bible reading. It is true that the Church has a strict discipline in regard to editions and translations of the Bible. Canon 1399 of the Code of Canon Law prohibits to Catholics the use of editions of original texts, ancient versions, and translations published by non-Catholics. The same code in Canon 1400 explicitly allows exception in the case of those who are "in any way" (*quovis modo*) engaged in theological or biblical studies, provided the editions in question are complete and do not attack Catholic doctrine in introductions or notes.

A momentary consideration of the history of vernacular translations may serve to show that this strict discipline is not founded on religious tyranny but on reasoned responsibility. The perennial concern of the Church is heresy, about which it cannot be indifferent. In the sixteenth century so reasonable a man as St. Thomas More found Tyndale's translation of certain words tendentious and heretical: *ecclesia* was translated by "congregation" instead of "church"; *presbuteros* by "elder" instead of "priest"; *gratia* by "favor" instead of "grace." More offensive still to Catholics were Tyndale's notes, which were described as "pestilent." The note on Numbers 23:8 ("How shall I curse whom God curseth not?") observed, "The Pope can tell how." This is a relatively mild example compared to others, which are better not quoted here.

The Church has not been opposed to vernacular translations as such. There was a complete translation of the Bible in French in the thirteenth century. Vernacular translations were established in Germany several centuries earlier. There were partial translations in Anglo-Saxon dating from Caedmon's metrical paraphrases in A.D. 670 and Bede's translation of the Fourth Gospel before A.D. 735. Considerable portions of the Old and New Testaments were available in translation in the tenth and eleventh centuries due particularly to the work of the Benedictine abbot Aelfric. The learned Abbot expressed some anxiety about the prudence of turning the Scriptures into the vernacular, an anxiety shared by other churchmen. That there were hazards in putting the Bible into the hands of the unlearned was proved a few centuries later with the Lollard Bible or the Bible of Wycliffe. Wycliffe made the Bible the ultimate and the only religious authority and attributed to every man, learned or ignorant, the right to examine it himself.

Centuries earlier St. Augustine (+A.D. 430) asked the question, "Do you want to know how heresies are produced?" And he answered it, "The Scriptures, which are good in themselves, were badly interpreted, and it was precisely this bad interpretation that men supported with audacity and assurance." It is fatal to divorce the book that is speechless from the Church that speaks. Theologically it cannot be a question of the Bible *or* the Church, or the

Church *versus* the Bible. In an exact theology it is the fact of the Bible *in* the Church. The New Testament is the witness to the living voice of the Church in the first century, and in every century it must exist in the vital continuity of the Christian tradition. This does not mean that interpretation will be frozen in a sort of static literalism. It must have that measure of flexibility that every living thing needs in order to survive.

The concept of the Bible in the Church ties in with the theology of the Church. It is intimately related to the existence of the Church expressed in sacramental life and worship. It is related to the Church in much more than an external relationship of authority. The Church's exercise of authority over the Bible rises out of the nature of the Church. It is the living voice of Christ in the world by virtue of the Spirit of Truth which abides with it forever according to his promise (John 14:16–17).

The Word of God in Scripture exists therefore as an organic part of the metaphysical unity of the Church. The Bible is also the object of investigation by the Church's scholars on the scientific level. Schools of higher biblical studies are the Pontifical Biblical Institute in Rome and the École Biblique in Jerusalem. The faculties of these schools are adorned with scholars of international prestige. The work of Père Roland de Vaux on the Dead Sea Scrolls is known the world over. In speaking of scholarly distinction the faculty of the University of Louvain is worthy of special mention. These schools publish learned biblical journals in which critical and exegetical questions are discussed at the highest levels. This interpretation is formally scientific and enjoys scientific authority. The Church on the other hand is the authentic interpreter of Scripture in virtue of a higher spiritual authority termed "dogmatic." Dogmatic authority exists in the Church in virtue of its mission from Christ as spiritual teacher of nations. It may come as a surprise to the reader to learn that in the course of its two thousand years the Church has defined dogmatically less than twenty texts of Scripture.

The following pages may bring home to the layman a fuller understanding of these things. It is the author's unpretentious hope that they will contribute in some measure to his understanding of the message of God in the Scriptures.

JOHN J. DOUGHERTY

*Feast of St. Thomas Aquinas*

# CONTENTS

# SEARCHING THE SCRIPTURES

# ONE

# THE BOOK THAT IS ONE
# AND MANY

Among the many titles given the Bible is the medieval one *Bibliotheca Sacra;* that is, Sacred Library. This title may serve to make the reader aware that the Bible is precisely that—a library or an anthology of sacred literature. Since we read printed Bibles, it is quite natural for us to think of the Bible as a book. In the time of Jesus one would not be apt to think of it as one book, since it was not a thing of printed pages bound together between boards, but a number of separate handwritten scrolls. This fact has been dramatically brought home by the recent discovery of the

Dead Sea Scrolls. The book of Isaias alone required one scroll.

The concept of the Bible as an anthology takes on greater significance when we consider the span of time involved in the composition of its books and their being gathered together to form a collection. Unlike, let us say, an edition of the complete works of Shakespeare in one volume, the Bible is not the work of one man, nor of one century, nor even of one millenium. The books of the Bible were composed by many individuals or schools over a period that spans more than a thousand years, when we consider the phase of oral tradition and early written documents. It must also be noted that the Bible was finished almost two thousand years ago. It comes down to this: when you read the Bible you are reading an ancient library of books written roughly between 1250 B.C. and A.D. 100. The significance behind these observations is that the world of the Bible was a cultural environment quite different from our own. It will bear the stamp of that environment.

Does it need saying that the surge and sweep of history have left their imprint on the Bible, that it is haunted by the ghosts of empires that rose and fell in its lifetime, that shadows of strange gods and alluring goddesses fall across its pages? To know nothing of this history is to miss much of the meaning of the Bible and the impact of its drama. To read the Bible without preparation is to read it in a vacuum, or in a fanciful world of one's own making. Either course is dangerous and may lead to a land of topsy-turvy interpretation. The inference is inescapable: some knowledge of the ancient world is an absolute prerequisite for intelligent Bible reading.

You might assume that you begin reading the Bible at the beginning and proceed progressively through the books in order. Let us look at this assumption. In our Bibles the books are arranged in categories, not in chronological order. The Old Testament is arranged in three sections, historical books, didactic books (moral instruction), and prophetic books. A similar division is found in the New Testament. It must be noted furthermore that the chronological order is not followed within the categories. Thus in the category of prophetic books Micheas (Micah) comes after Jeremias, although the former is several centuries earlier than the latter. In the New Testament St. Paul's epistles to the Thessalonians come toward the end of the collection, although they are probably the earliest of his letters. Now it is altogether obvious that to follow the history of divine revelation the chronology of its records must be established. Consequently some rearranging of the books according to a chronological scheme is desirable, and the best way to read the Bible is not from beginning to end, but according to a plan.

Since books in one category are related in time to those in another category, the plan would call for some measure of co-ordination of related parts. For example, the book of Jeremias in the prophetic category should be correlated to the period of his activity, the history of the last days of

Juda as related in 2 Kings; the letters of St. Paul should be read in chronological order against the background of the Acts of the Apostles. This kind of manipulation may seem bothersome to the reader, but it will certainly contribute to his understanding of the messages of Jeremias and Paul.

The re-ordering of the books of the Bible does not stop there. Biblical scholars apply the norms of literary criticism to the Scriptures. Literary criticism is the study of the vocabulary, grammar, and style of the books in the languages of their original composition, namely, Hebrew, Aramaic, and Greek. The content of the book is analyzed to determine the character of its composition, whether it is the work of one author or a compilation from different sources. The historical and geographical data of the book are examined for clues to the time of composition. The application of literary criticism to the Bible is of comparatively recent date. The science as such is quite valid and does not imply of itself any disrespect for the Word of God. An illustration may serve to show how it applies. In the book of Ecclesiastes the author speaks in the person of King Solomon. If we accept that at face value, the book must be dated in the tenth century B.C. The internal evidence of the book, such as the Aramaic coloring of the language (Aramaic comes late in Israel's history) and the ideology, point to a time long after Solomon; namely, the period of Hellenism—that is, after 334 B.C. The critic concludes that the book was written about 300/200 B.C. and that the author assumed the name of King Solomon as a pseudonym, a literary custom quite acceptable in antiquity.

The science of biblical criticism examines individual books in terms of unity or composite character. A noteworthy example of this is the analysis of the Book of Isaias. From a study of internal criteria—that is, style, historical references, and theological concepts—critics conclude that the book as we know it is not the work of one author, but rather of three. The first part (Chapters 1–35) they attribute to Isaias, the eighth-century prophet. The second (40–55) and third (56–66) parts are attributed to unknown authors of the school of Isaias writing at the time of the Exile and after, late in the sixth century. Although at first hearing the lay reader may consider such maneuvers pointless and far from spiritual devotion, a moment's reflection will bring home to him that the history of revelation cannot be reconstructed without proper evaluation of the sources of that history. The restless quest of the biblical critic merits our respectful attention.

It cannot be denied that the science of literary criticism has contributed to our understanding of the Bible. An even greater contribution has been made by the science of archeology. In what does its contribution consist? The answer to that question is large, but an illustration may serve as answer for the moment. When Israel invaded Canaan the inhabitants of the land, the Canaanites, constituted a constant threat to the purity of their religion and their faith in the Lord. Would we not be in a better position to understand that conflict if we knew the religion of the Canaanites? In 1929 at Ras Shamra (Ugarit) a library of Phoenician literature was discovered, firsthand records of the religion of a people culturally one with the Canaanites. The data of those documents have thrown much light on the religious culture of Canaan and consequently clarified the meaning of many Old Testament texts.

Archeology has contributed information on the language of the Bible, on its legal customs and its literature. It is the handmaid of history. Excavations in Mesopotamia and Egypt, as well as Palestine, have greatly increased our knowledge of Israel's neighbors, their civilizations and religious cultures, their art and architecture. The Bible is no longer our sole source of information on ancient Israel. Information comes directly, for example, from the prism of Sennacherib, indirectly from the tablets of Nuzi in Mesopotamia. These throw light on the legal customs of the patriarchs of Genesis.

What are the implications of this knowledge for proper interpretation of the Bible? Again let us turn to an example. Take the story of the Flood in Genesis 6–9. That story stood in splendid solitude in the Bible until the close of the nineteenth century. In 1872 in excavations at ancient Nineveh, George Smith uncovered many cuneiform tablets. When deciphered they turned up a Babylonian flood story that showed marked similarity to the narrative in Genesis. True, it was pagan and polytheistic to the core, but what about it? Did Genesis borrow the story from

Babylonia and eliminate the mythology? Was there really a great flood and total destruction of the human race? These were the inevitable questions the discovery stirred up. Neither the biblical scholar nor the Bible reader can ignore such questions. To do so would be to abandon reason. On the other hand, to deny the divine authority of the Bible because of them would be to abandon faith. There is another alternative, namely, to reread the Bible in light of the ancient literatures and determine precisely what it does and does not affirm.

A most important aspect of archeological discoveries for biblical studies lies in the literatures of ancient peoples— the literature of the Egyptians in hieroglyphics, that of the Sumerians, Babylonians, and Assyrians in cuneiform. The deciphering of these ancient languages is one of the great conquests of the human mind. What significance does this have for the Bible? It means that we possess writings composed in the same period as the books of the Old Testament, writings from the same cultural environment, and some in languages closely related to biblical Hebrew.[1] And what do we learn from the comparison? We understand better the literary forms we meet in the Bible. Understanding the forms, we are in a better position to interpret the Bible correctly. Again an example may serve to bring out the point. How are we to understand the serpent in the Genesis story of Eden? Documents from the ancient Near

[1] Cf. *The Ancient Near East: An Anthology of Texts and Pictures,* edited by J. B. Pritchard (Princeton University Press, 1958).

East and cultic art inform us on the significant role of the serpent in the fertility rites of ancient paganism. As a result we are in a better position to determine the author's motivation in depicting the tempter in Eden as a serpent.

Does it not seem that all this provides us with material for a more objective approach to biblical interpretation? A better knowledge of the Old World will lead to better knowledge of the old book that came from it, the Bible. This method is security, too, against emotional or irrational interpretations. The importance of this phase of biblical study has been stressed by Pope Pius XII in his encyclical on biblical studies (*Divino Afflante Spiritu*, September 30, 1953). "The literal sense of a passage is not always as obvious in the speeches and writings of ancient authors of the East, as it is in the works of our own time. For what they wished to express is not to be determined by the rules of grammar and philology alone, nor solely by the context; the interpreter must, as it were, go back wholly in spirit to those remote centuries of the East and with the aid of history, archeology, ethnology, and other sciences, accurately determine what modes of writing, so to speak, the authors of that ancient period would be likely to use, and in fact did use.

"For the ancient peoples of the East, in order to express their ideas, did not always employ those kinds of speech which we use today; but rather *those used by the men of their times and countries*. What those exactly were the commentator cannot determine as it were in advance, but *only after a careful examination of the ancient literature of the East."* (Emphasis supplied.)

The principle of interpretation referred to in this excerpt is technically termed "literary genre." The reader is familiar with the literary genres of our own day: the short story, the novel, the poem, the ballad, and so on. He is not ordinarily familiar with the literary genres of the ancient Near East. Archeological excavators have brought to light thousands of ancient documents. These supply examples of the literary forms of antiquity and this knowledge helps place biblical texts in their historical perspective.

The considerations thus far may give the reader the impression that the Bible is strongly marked with diversity. The impression is not false. The Sacred Library is marked by a diversity of themes and a multiplicity of authors, viewed from the human and historical point of view. From the theological point of view it is marked by a singular unity. This overarching unity rises out of the fact of divine inspiration. God is author of all the Bible.

The idea of divine authorship or inspiration was a central doctrine of pre-Christian Judaism. This doctrine of Jewish faith was accepted by Jesus and his Apostles. The most formal statement of it appears in St. Paul's Second Epistle to Timothy. "From thy infancy thou hast known the Sacred Writings, which are able to instruct thee unto salvation by the faith which is in Christ Jesus. *All Scripture is inspired by God* and useful for teaching, for reproving, for correcting, for instructing in justice; that the man of God may be perfect, equipped for every good work" (3:15–17). (Emphasis supplied.)

The words of St. Paul apply to the books of the Old Testament, as the context shows. When the New Testament writings made their appearance they were read in Christian assemblies alongside the Old Testament. In his preaching Jesus had accepted the Old Testament, but had made himself master of it, as is clear from the Sermon on the Mount (Matt. 5–7). In imitation of the Master the first Christians considered the Gospel the "fulfillment" of "the Law and the Prophets," that is, of the Old Testament. The authority of Christ lived on in his Gospel as preached by the Apostles. The apostolic authority passed over to their writings when they came into existence, and it was not long before the New Testament books were placed beside those of the Old Testament as divinely inspired. This is already suggested for the Pauline epistles in 2 Peter 3:16, where they are compared to "the rest of the Scriptures."

The faith of the Church in this doctrine never wavered. It is witnessed to from Pope Clement, who died in A.D. 96, to Pope Pius XII, who died in 1958. The late Holy Father in his encyclical on Sacred Scripture (*Divino Afflante Spiritu*) quoted the Vatican Council's words, which describe the Scriptures as books that, "having been written under the inspiration of the Holy Spirit, have God for their author."

In the traditional theology of the Church, inspiration is a supernatural reality that places the books of the Bible in a unique position outside all natural categories. The book is the "Word of God" for the reason that it has God for its author. Inextricably linked with this doctrine and flowing from it is the concept that the Scriptures are free from error, the doctrine of biblical inerrancy. As long as the world of the Bible-reader was identical with the world of the biblical authors there was no problem. As long as men accepted that the sun moved across the heavens they saw no problem in the words of Josue, "Stand still, O Sun" (Josue 10:12). To a man like Galileo, who helped to change the concept of the world, they did present a problem. The problem reached its peak in the late nineteenth century and the early twentieth. It was occasioned by the tremendous growth of human knowledge due to advances in the physical sciences and history.

The doctrines of biblical inspiration and inerrancy staggered under the impact of the new knowledge about the age of the world and the origin of species. There came to pass a great conflict between religion and science. Rationalistic philosophies had their heyday, and at length Modernism reared its head to threaten the very foundations of the Christian faith. Theologians rallied to the defense of doctrine with such devices as limiting biblical inspiration to matters of faith and morals, or restricting inerrancy to things taught as opposed to things said. The Church judged such limitations unacceptable and reaffirmed that "it was absolutely wrong and forbidden either to narrow inspiration to certain parts only of Holy Scripture or to admit that the sacred writer had erred" (Leo XIII, *Prov. Deus*).

The Bible survived the crisis and in our day has come to see its second spring. As sciences had shaken it in the nineteenth century, a science supported it wondrously in the twentieth: the science of archeology. In a calmer atmosphere and a changed philosophical climate theologians and exegetes work at the existing problems. Some acquaintance with this historical background is necessary to understand the changes that have taken place in biblical interpretation and the new directions of research. Exegesis was forced to make certain adjustments. An example comes immediately to mind. According to Archbishop Usher's chronological note on Genesis 1:1 the world was created in B.C. 4004. Such a statement is preposterous today. The late Pope Pius XII shared the opinion that creation began some five billion years ago.

The religious authority of the Bible is founded upon the fact of its divine inspiration. When traditional Christian theology speaks of the Bible as the Word of God it is more than a figure of speech. It is a reality of faith. By the same token a rational theology must subject the concept of inspiration to careful analysis and define precisely the borders of biblical authority. It excludes at once the mechanistic notion of biblical inspiration as a process of dictation from God to man. It excludes likewise the concept that reduces inspiration to the natural order of Divine Providence, making inspiration the coincidence of the historical event and the enlightened mind to interpret it. Traditional theology affirms that God is author in a true but analogous sense.

There is a seeming paradox in the statement that God and man are authors of the same book. The paradox is not resolved by thinking of them as co-authors like Gilbert and Sullivan. It is resolved by conceiving the relationship between God and man as one of instrumental co-operation. An example of instrumental co-operation on the natural level is the pianist at the piano. The piano is the instrument, the pianist is the principal cause, the concerto is the effect. In the process of playing, the piano is elevated by the action of the pianist to produce an effect that is beyond its proper capacity. Similarly God can use a man to produce an effect that is beyond the capacity of man. A man can produce a human book; he cannot produce a divine book except under immediate divine influence. God can use a man instrumentally by a direct interior influence on his intellect and will so that the result, the book, proceeds both from God and from man.

With these observations in mind the following official statement of the Church will be better understood: "By supernatural power, He so moved and impelled them to write—He so assisted them when writing—that the things which He ordered, and those only, they, first, rightly understood, then willed faithfully to write down, and finally expressed in apt words and with infallible truth. Otherwise it could not be said that He was the Author of the entire Scriptures" (Leo XIII, *Prov. Deus*).

The problem of biblical inerrancy is a thorny one. It is a different problem for the contemporary scholar than it was for Augustine or Aquinas because of our increased knowledge of the biblical world and biblical times. Leo XIII laid down certain principles in *Providentissimus Deus*. For example, the human author cannot be accused of error when he speaks about the physical world according to appearances. In his encyclical *Divino Afflante Spiritu* Pius XII placed great emphasis on the function of literary genre in this connection. The truth of a passage or book must be judged in view of the genre. The Pope emphasized that "the supreme rule of interpretation is to discover and define what the writer intended to express," and it is the determination of the genre that helps us discern the writer's intention.

The doctrines of inspiration and inerrancy are engaging the attention of Catholic theologians at the present time. The latter calls for theological development. An interesting effort in this direction may be seen in the recent study of Père Benoit of the École Biblique.[2] He calls attention to the difference between the Greco-Roman and the Semitic outlook. "If we seek in the Bible a statement of speculative 'truths,' a collection of doctrines, we approach it as Greco-Latins. But it is as Semites that we must open this book to meet God in it, such as he gives himself to us—a God who acts, enters into our history, speaks to our hearts, who cer-

[2] Cf. *Initiation Biblique*, 3d. ed., A. Robert and A. Tricot, (Paris, 1954), pp. 6–45.

tainly 'reveals' himself to our knowledge, but by a way of life which calls for in response a knowledge made of love, of obedience, of total engagement. There is here a whole problem that does not correspond to our Western formation. It is imperatively necessary for us to immerse ourselves in it, if we wish to read the Holy Book as it needs to be read—not in order to find in it what it does not offer us and be scandalized, but to seek in it what it does offer us and by this to live."

# TWO

# THE BOOK OF DIVERS TONGUES

In the Bible God speaks in three languages, Hebrew, Aramaic, and Greek. These are the languages in which the books of the Bible were originally written. The reasons for this are to be found in the historical circumstances. By far the greater part of the Old Testament was written in Hebrew. The Hebrew people were Semites, and their language belongs to the family of Semitic languages spoken in the ancient Near East. The remote racial roots of the Hebrews go back to the desert of Arabia, whence they migrated to Ur, perhaps in the third millennium B.C. In the patriarchal period their family ties were in Haran in the region of Aram. The Hebrew dialect at the time of the conquest of Canaan in the thirteenth century B.C. may be described as Arabo-Aramaic. It was influenced by the dialect of Canaan after the conquest. These three strains blend to form the language of the Old Testament, biblical Hebrew.

Archeology has supplied us with contemporary witnesses to the Hebrew of the Old Testament. One of these is the Siloam inscription. A tunnel extends beneath Jerusalem from the Gihon spring, on the eastern slopes of the city, to where once stood the pool of Siloam. The tunnel was cut during the reign of King Ezechias (716–687 B.C.). In 1880 a boy wading in the pool found the inscription in the rock wall of the tunnel, a memorial to the completion of the work of "boring through." The inscription was cut out and placed in the Imperial Ottoman Museum in Constantinople. It exemplifies the Hebrew language and script in the time of Isaias the prophet. Excavations on the site of Samaria, capital of the northern kingdom of Israel, provided more evidence of the language and script in the Samaritan ostraca. These are inscribed potsherds dating very likely from the time of Jeroboam II (783–743 B.C.). Another notable witness are the Lachish letters discovered in 1935 and 1938 during work on the mound at Lachish in southern Palestine. They date from 588 B.C., the year Nabuchodonosor began the siege of Jerusalem, in the days of the prophet Jeremias. These documents are all written in an ancient script that differs from the square form of the letters in later use; the latter is really an Aramaic script. Aramaic replaced Hebrew as the language of the Jews after the Exile (586 B.C.). This explains why some later parts of the Old Testament are written in Aramaic, notably in the books of Esdras and Daniel. Aramaic was the language Jesus spoke. It is a Semitic dialect, being related to Hebrew somewhat as Italian is to French.

The reader may ask what all this has to do with reading the Bible in English. It will serve to remind him that he is reading a translation of ancient books. But more than this, we may note that language is not merely a matter of words. Every language has its own idiom, its imagery, its distinctive color. It is a vehicle of ideas and emotions. The genius of a language is related to the temperament and mentality of the people who speak it. Their mind and their heart is in their tongue. This must perforce show through even in translations. Our English speech is marked by Hebrew idioms, Hebraisms of the early translations. Such are "Holy of Holies," "Song of Songs," "King of Kings." These Hebrew idioms are really equivalent to English superlatives. Such inversions as "man of sorrows" or "oil of gladness" are also due to Hebrew influence.

Hebrew imagery comes through in translation and will at times startle the reader into the realization that this is a book from an old and different world. It is hard to imagine an American writer describing the earthquake at Sinai in this fashion:

> The mountains skipped like rams,
>     and the hills like lambs of the flock.
>             (Ps. 113 [114]:4)

Or can you imagine a poet of the Western world casting his romantic verse in this mold?

> Your hair is like a flock of goats,
>     streaming down from Galaad.
> Your teeth are like a flock of ewes
>     which came up from the washing.
>             (Cant. 6:5 f.)

The Hebrew Old Testament has the unmistakable complexion of the ancient East: "the shadowed livery of the burnished sun."

The original copies of the books of the Hebrew Old Testament have all perished. The oldest witnesses to the originals are the manuscripts, copies made by hand through the long centuries before the invention of printing. Old manuscripts are more than curiosities and collectors' items for the biblical scholar. They are the scientific tools of his trade. Manuscripts differ from one another because of mistakes or changes made by copyists. At times efforts were made to correct and revise manuscripts, and thus a type of text would arise that is called a recension. The study of manuscripts for the purpose of restoring the original text as far as possible is called textual criticism. Let us consider now some of the Hebrew manuscripts, and see the importance of the Dead Sea Scrolls in this connection.

The oldest complete manuscript of the Hebrew Bible was preserved in the Synagogue of the Sephardim in Aleppo. Its date was about A.D. 950. Unfortunately it was destroyed during the recent troubles in Syria. Professor Kahle had earlier established the fact that Codex 19a of the Leningrad Library is a good copy of it, made in A.D. 1008. These and all medieval Hebrew manuscripts reflect a common recension, a text that was fixed as the official text of Judaism about A.D. 100. This type of text is called the Masoretic Text because of the work of the "men of tradition," the Masoretes; *masorah* is the Hebrew word for "tradition." Their prodigious labors made possible a practically immutable transmission of the Masoretic Hebrew Bible.

The discovery of the Dead Sea Scrolls revolutionized the study of the Hebrew text. Prior to the discovery very little existed in the way of early manuscript evidence. The oldest known were the Nash papyrus, a fragment containing the Ten Commandments and the Shema (Deut. 6:4), dating from the second or first century before Christ, and some fragments of about the seventh century A.D. discovered in the Old Cairo Geniza. (A Geniza is the place where they store old manuscripts). Complete Hebrew manuscripts, as just observed, dated from the tenth century or later. The picture changed with dramatic suddenness with the discoveries at Wady Qumran.

The first scrolls were discovered in 1947. Two of them proved to be copies of Isaias. There was much debate about the date of the scrolls, but it is now quite generally accepted that they are from the second/first century B.C. Observe what this means! The Qumran Isaias is a thousand years older than the Masoretic manuscripts described above. Since the original discovery in 1947 other caves at Qumran have given up fragments of biblical manuscripts. From Cave IV there are copies of Exodus and Samuel from the third century B.C.; of Deuteronomy, Isaias, the Minor Prophets, Job, and Psalms from the second century B.C. The significance of this discovery for the study of the text of the Hebrew Bible is incalculable. The manuscripts represent a different recension from that of the Masoretes, one akin to the recension used by the translators of the Greek Old Testament, the Septuagint.

This earliest translation of the Hebrew Bible was done at Alexandria roughly in the period between 250 and 100 B.C. The city was founded in 332 B.C. by Alexander the Great in the course of his victorious march eastward. It soon had a large Jewish population, and the fact that they spoke only Greek gave rise to the need for a translation.

There is extant a certain *Letter of Aristeas* that pretends to give an account of the undertaking. This dates from 100 B.C. Aristeas professes to be a courtier of King Philadelphus (285–247 B.C.). The letter is shot through with legendary details, but from it came the traditional name of the translation. It is called the Septuagint (Seventy) because the letter states that the translation of the Pentateuch was the work of seventy men, actually seventy-two. The historical fact seems to be that the Septuagint translation is the work of different hands beginning with the translation of the Pentateuch in the third century. It was probably completed before the first century B.C., as suggested by the prologue to Jesus Sirach. It soon came to be used by all Greek-speaking Jews throughout the Mediterranean world.

Manuscript fragments of the Septuagint were found in Cave IV at Qumran, fragments of Leviticus and Numbers from the first century B.C. or early first century A.D. In the John Rylands Library at Manchester, England, there is a papyrus fragment of Deuteronomy from about 150 B.C. It was recovered from a mummy cartonnage. Parts of eight Old Testament books are preserved in the Chester Beatty papyri of the second and third centuries A.D. These were purchased in Egypt and brought to England by Chester Beatty. There is a third-century papyrus of the Minor Prophets in the Freer Collection in Washington, D.C., and the most complete manuscript of all is the handsome fourth-century parchment in the Vatican. From the same Christian century comes the Sinai Codex of the British Museum.

This Alexandrian version, or Septuagint, was the Old Testament of the early Church. It is the version ordinarily quoted by the New Testament writers, and as the Hebrew Bible left its mark on our language, so too did the Septuagint. Words in our language like paraclete, baptism, anathema, are Greek words transliterated. The version enjoyed great esteem among the Church Fathers and not infrequently was considered inspired. The idea of the inspiration of the Septuagint has been recently revived by Père Benoit in the study referred to in the preceeding chapter.

The explanation of the fact that the Catholic Old Testament differs in content from the Protestant and Jewish is to be found in the Septuagint version. The precise contents of the Alexandrian collection or canon at the time of Christ is somewhat uncertain, as is that of the canon of the Jews of Palestine. However, it is certain that the Alexandrian Septuagint did include certain books not in the Hebrew collection. The first Christian missionaries had made use of the Septuagint in bringing the Gospel to the Greek-speaking pagan world. It was the Bible of the primitive Church. The question of its relationship to the Palestinian canon was not brought up until the second century, by Melito of Sardis (+c. A.D. 180). By this time the Palestinian canon had been standardized and there were seven books not included in it that were part of the Alexandrian canon. They were Tobias, Judith, Wisdom, Sirach, Baruch, 1–2 Machabees, plus portions of Esther (10:4–16:24) and Daniel (3:24–90; 13; 14). The debate concerning the canonicity and consequently the inspiration of these books continued among the Fathers for several centuries, with a man like Jerome opposing them and his contemporary Augustine defending them. Official pronouncements of the churches did not come until the close of the fourth century in the Councils of Rome (A.D. 382) and North Africa, at Hippo

(A.D. 393) and Carthage (A.D. 397). They list the canon of Old Testament books according to the Septuagint.

The question was rarely discussed again until the Reformation. Luther and the sixteenth-century reformers took the Hebrew Bible as their norm and excluded the seven books, which were termed Apocrypha. The Council of Trent, epitome of Rome's Counter Reformation, declared in a decree of faith that the books are inspired and part of the canon of the Old Testament. They are called deutero-canonical books by Catholics by reason of the fact that universal recognition came later in the Church.

We come now to the New Testament. With the exception of Matthew's Gospel, which was written in Aramaic originally, the books of the New Testament were written in Greek. It was the Greek spoken by the common man in the Near East after the cultural expansion of Hellenism. For this reason it is called Koiné or common Greek. The terminology of the New Testament was influenced by the Septuagint, and its style is colored by the Aramaic background of the Apostles, notably in Matthew and John. The problem of the New Testament Greek text is not as involved as the text of the Old Testament, because the books were written in the course of one generation, not over a period of a thousand years. The manuscript witnesses are closer to the originals in time. This may be dramatically shown by pointing to the John Rylands Library papyrus of the Fourth Gospel, a fragment containing a few verses, dated in the early second century, about A.D. 125. This is very close to

John's time. He died probably between A.D. 90 and 100.

Over a hundred pages of the Greek New Testament are preserved in the Chester Beatty papyri dating from the early third century. A papyrus manuscript of the Gospel of John was published in 1956 and 1958. It is Papyrus Bodmer II, and is considered the most important manuscript published since the publication of the Chester Beatty papyri in 1933–34. The Bodmer papyrus is better preserved than any other New Testament manuscript. Its date is placed about A.D. 200. From the fourth century and after come the great parchment manuscripts like the Codex Vaticanus, the Sinaiticus, and the Alexandrinus. Altogether there are more than four thousand manuscript witnesses to the New Testament text in whole or in part. It is the best authenticated book of antiquity, and we can be sure that our New Testaments are practically identical with the originals.

Rome ruled the world when the Gospel was first preached, but it was not preached in the tongue of the Romans, for Rome's domination was political. Hellenism was still the dominant culture. Greek remained the language of the Church until the middle of the third century. The first Latin translations made their appearance toward the end of the second century in North Africa and southern Gaul. From that time on Latin translations increased. The manuscript witnesses to these are called the Old Latin, as opposed to Vulgate manuscripts.

*Vulgata* is the title given the Latin translation of Jerome,

which he completed about A.D. 405. "Vulgate" is equivalent
to our expression "commonly received version." It is impossible to exaggerate the significance of the work of the great
humanist St. Jerome. He first revised the Latin New Testament at Rome at the request of Pope Damasus (+A.D.
384), and later at Bethlehem he translated the Hebrew
Bible into Latin. The Latin Vulgate of the Roman Church
is almost totally the work of Jerome. It was the Bible of
Western civilization for a thousand years, a foundation
stone of the medieval culture, the inspiration of its artists,
the handbook of its scholars. Its mark can be seen in the
Loggia of Raphael or in the windows of Chartres Cathedral.
It begot an art tradition of its own in illuminated manuscripts, such Celtic masterpieces as the Lindisfarne Gospels
and the Book of Kells. The anonymous artist of the latter
has been compared to Michelangelo in genius. Nor can we
forget to mention the charming books of hours, like the
*Belles Heures* of Jean, Duke of Berry, Prince of France,
recently reproduced by the Metropolitan Museum of Art.

The Vulgate received its greatest distinction at the Council of Trent in 1546. The Council declared it the authentic
Latin version. The decree was misunderstood by some,
who stated that the Council declared the Vulgate inspired. Such was not the case. The intention of the Council
is clear from the context of the decree and from the discus-
sions of the theologians as recorded in the Acts of the
Council. The word "authentic" in the decree has a juridical
sense and means that the Vulgate is trustworthy in matters

of faith and morals. The reason for this "authenticity" in the words of the decree is its "long use of many centuries in the Church." The guarantee that it is reliable in matters of faith and morals is its relation to the infallible Church. It was not declared critically authentic, that is, superior to the Hebrew and Greek texts.

The English translation made for Catholics at Rheims and Douay was based on the Latin Vulgate. Catholics forced to flee England during the persecutions of Elizabeth settled in France and Flanders. William Allen of Oxford, later Cardinal, founded the English College at Douay for the training of priests. The translation was the work of the College faculty, particularly Gregory Martin. Because of political troubles in Flanders the college had to move to Rheims for a time, and so it happened that the translation of the New Testament was published there in 1582. The Old Testament was published much later at Douay, in 1609–10. The translation was produced amid the tensions of religious persecution and tendentious vernacular translations of heretical sects. These conditions contributed to the translators' almost slavish adherence to the Latin. An example of this Latinate style may be seen in Ephesians 6:12: "Against the spirituals of wickedness in the celestials." This situation was remedied a century and a half later when the Douay-Rheims Bible was revised by Dr. Challoner (1749–50). Dr. Challoner modernized the language and style, and at times substituted readings from the King James Version. This revision of the Douay-Rheims was to remain the Bible of English-speaking Catholics for some two hundred years.

The crown and culmination of the many Protestant English versions of the sixteenth century was the King James version of 1611, the Authorized Version. It is a monument of classic English style, "a miracle and a landmark." Its critical value is by no means up to its style, due to the fact that the science of textual criticism was not developed at the time. This science classifies and evaluates the manuscript evidence. In establishing a text of the Old or New Testament it considers not only the Hebrew and Greek manuscripts, but the ancient versions as well. Thus it was possible that the Latin Vulgate might have certain readings that were better than those of the Greek manuscripts of the New Testament used by the translators of the King James version. An example of this is seen in the doxology added to the Our Father in Matthew 6:13: "For thine is the kingdom and the power and the glory forever." This addition is not found in the Latin Vulgate, and consequently it is not in the Rheims New Testament. It is not found in the better Greek manuscripts, and it must be judged as a gloss, not part of the original Lord's Prayer. It was this critical inferiority that led to the demand for a revision of the Authorized Version. The Revised Version was published in England in 1881–85. The American Standard Edition of the Revised Version appeared in 1901.

The twentieth century is like the sixteenth in the fact that it is producing a host of Bible translations. The new

Protestant translation, the Revised Standard Version, appeared in 1946 (New Testament) and 1952 (Old Testament). This is a translation based on the original languages. It stands in relation to the King James and the Revised Version as a revision, as declared on the title pages: "being the version set forth A.D 1611, revised A.D. (1881-) 1885 and A.D. 1901, compared with the most ancient authorities and revised A.D. 1946 (1952)." Its chief value consists in its critical superiority to the earlier versions, due to the advances in textual criticism and biblical science generally.

On the Catholic side there is the revision of the Challoner-Rheims New Testament that was published in 1941. This work was undertaken under the patronage of the Episcopal Committee of the Confraternity of Christian Doctrine, which explains why it is familiarly referred to as the Confraternity edition. It is the work of members of the Catholic Biblical Association of America. The basic text of of the revision was the Latin Vulgate, not the Greek text. This anachronism is being remedied, since a new translation from the Greek is in progress. The Confraternity Old Testament is a translation from the Hebrew or Greek texts. At this time two volumes have appeared, Volume i, Genesis–Ruth, and Volume iii, Job–Sirach.

The most dramatic case of contemporary Bible translation is the work of the late Msgr. Ronald Knox. Singlehanded he produced over a period of nine years a "new translation." The New Testament was published in 1946, the Old Testament in 1948 and 1950. Here, too, the translation is based on the Latin Vulgate. The reason for this is that the translation conforms to the liturgical texts of the Mass and the Breviary, which are from the Vulgate. The style of the "Knox Bible" marks a real departure from the familiar diction of the King James or the Douay-Rheims. The purpose of Msgr. Knox was to turn out a translation in "timeless English." The criticism most frequently leveled against his translation is that it runs too often into paraphrase. There is validity in this criticism. No one can say now how long the Knox version and other contemporary translations will endure, but we may say that they will have an influence on the English translations yet to come.

# THREE

# A FRAME FOR THE BIBLICAL PICTURE

There is history in the Bible, but it is not a history book in the ordinary sense of the word. What interested the ancient Israelite was the meaning of the event. He saw in events the expression of a plan, a design of God. The Bible's chief concern is not the affairs of men as such, but God's entrance into the affairs of men. Its primary theme is the wondrous works of God, wrought of old for Israel, and "in the fullness of time" for all mankind. God's instruments in the performance of his wondrous deeds were the might of the storm, the death-dealing plague, or the dread Assyrian army.

Men were his primary instruments, men like Moses the Hebrew or Cyrus the Persian. The Bible has much to say about Moses, little to say about Cyrus. The reader must supplement the comparative silence of the Bible with some knowledge of profane history. For fuller understanding he must place the Sacred Library in the frame of history and geography.

The Bible lands extend from the Persian Gulf in Asia to the delta of the Nile in Egyptian Africa, up through Turkey, once Asia Minor, on through Greece and the islands of the Mediterranean to Rome. The stage of Old Testament history was the area between the Persian Gulf and the Nile, a region marked by the contrast of desert and fertility. Egypt's fertility is the gift of the Nile that floods the land regularly each year. A narrow corridor of fertility skirts the river. Beyond this stretch uninhabitable deserts. The name Mesopotamia means the land "between the rivers." Fertility there is the gift of the Tigris and Euphrates. Between these areas extend the coastlands of the eastern Mediterranean: Palestine—now Israel—and Syria. This region owes its fertility to the winter rainfalls. This whole region is like a great green patch on the surrounding deserts, shaped like a half-moon. It has been aptly named the Fertile Crescent.

The desert of Arabia was the home of the Semites. Time and again through the centuries hordes of nomads from the desert invaded the fertile crescent where the old civilizations were established. Among these invading hordes were

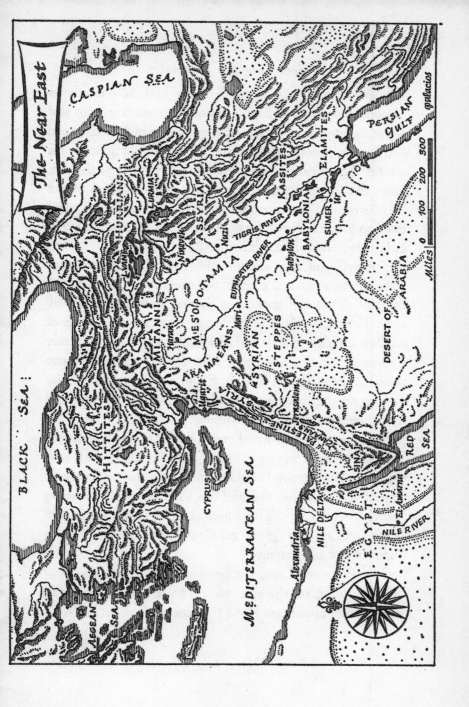

the ancestors of Abraham. To the east and north of Mesopotamia rose the highlands of what are now Iran and Armenia, populated by Indo-European peoples who surged down at intervals to despoil the land or to dominate it for a time. The Syro-Palestine coastland lay open to the sea. From the islands of the Aegean came the invasion of the Peoples of the Sea, among them the Philistines. Their name lived on in the name of the land. The Greeks called it *Syria-Palaistine*, Syria of the Philistines.

The valley of the Nile and the Tigris-Euphrates valley were the two cultural centers of antiquity. The latter was the seat of the civilizations of Sumer, Babylonia, and Assyria. Palestine was situated between these two centers of civilization like a bridge and a highroad. Although the early history of Israel is associated with Egypt, and Moses was raised in the court of Pharaoh, Egypt did not exert great influence on the culture of Israel. The evidence of the Old Testament points rather to Mesopotamian influence. In the period of nationhood Israel was a buffer state between the warring powers of Egypt and Mesopotamia, and very often the battleground of their armies. In the lull between imperialistic marches the land was a harbor and a sanctuary for wandering tribes. There nomad Israel found a promised home, where two great religious cultures were born: Judaism and Christianity.

The Promised Land lay between the sea on the west and the desert on the east, some 150 miles long and 125 miles wide, about one third the size of Pennsylvania. Its most striking physical feature is the Jordan depression. This gorge was once the bed of an inland sea, two remnants of which are the lake called Galilee and the Dead Sea. The heart-shaped lake of Galilee has great charm and loveliness, especially in the spring when wild flowers of many colors cover the hills around it. On the north shore of the lake ruins of a synagogue mark the site of Capharnaum, where Jesus made his home. He preached the Sermon on the Mount on a hillside overlooking the lake and spoke from a boat swayed gently by its waters. Between the lake and the Dead Sea the Jordan River runs its tortuous course. Not far from the point where it enters the Dead Sea, John the Baptist preached the coming of the kingdom, and there Jesus came to be baptized. Jericho is situated not far away, and south of it are the caves of Wady Qumran where the Dead Sea Scrolls were found.

The Dead Sea is a strange sea. It lies almost thirteen hundred feet below sea level in a sun-bleached arid waste. Its waters have six times the salt content of the ocean. Many legends are linked to it. On its shore stands a column of rock salt men call Lot's wife. Fish die on entering its waters, but birds can fly over it in safety, despite contrary legends. Sodom and Gomorrha sleep beneath its waters.

Mountain ranges flank the Jordan Valley on either side. To the east rises the Transjordan plateau, beautiful pastoral heights once the land of Galaad, Ammon, and Moab. To the south of the Dead Sea lay the land of Edom. The western ridge is the spine of the region this side of the

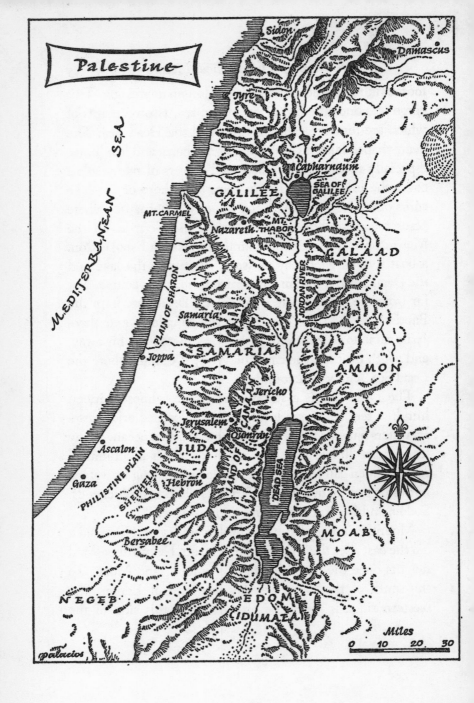

# Palestine

Sidon

Damascus

Tyre

MT. CARMEL

GALILEE

Capharnaum

SEA OF GALILEE

Nazareth

MT. THABOR

GALAAD

MEDITERRANEAN SEA

PLAIN OF SHARON

Samaria

Joppa

SAMARIA

AMMON

Jericho

LAND OF CANAAN

Jerusalem

Qumran

Ascalon

JUDA

Gaza

SHEPHELAH

Hebron

DEAD SEA

PHILISTINE PLAIN

Bersabee

MOAB

NEGEB

EDOM

(IDUMAEA)

Palacios

Miles

0    10    20    30

Jordan. It is broken in Galilee by the Plain of Esdraelon, named from the ancient royal city of Jezrael. A spur of the ridge juts out to the sea in Mount Carmel, redolent with memories of Elias the prophet. To the east of the plain are the slopes of Mount Gelboe where Saul and Jonathan died in battle against the Philistines. In the heart of the plain Mount Thabor rises dramatically. Not far away is lovely Nazareth. Samaria, capital of the northern kingdom of Israel, lies on the ridge further to the south. In the Judaean sector of the western plateau are situated Jerusalem, Bethlehem five miles below it, and further south Hebron, where Abraham is buried and where David was first named king. Beyond Hebron to the south lie Bersabee (Beersheba) the Negeb, and the desert of Sinai where Israel wandered for forty years and Moses received the Law.

Between the western plateau and the sea stretches the maritime plain. Below Mount Carmel it was called the Plain of Saron (Sharon), renowned for its fertilty and beauty. The coast town of Jaffa (Joppa) was in this region. South of this lay the Sephela (Shephelah), also called the Plain of Philistia. Here were situated the towns of the Philistines, like Geth and Ascalon. This region was the setting for the exploits of Samson and the contest between David and Goliath.[1]

Biblical history proper begins with Abraham. His native

[1] An indispensable book for the student of the Bible is a biblical atlas. *Atlas of the Bible* by L. H. Grollenberg, o.p. (Nelson, 1956) is an excellent combination of maps, illustrations, and text.

city was Ur, situated at the head of the Persian Gulf, near the eastern tip of the Fertile Crescent. From there the family migrated to Haran on the upper Euphrates. In Abraham's day the great glory of Ur was behind it. It had been the capital of the Sumerian kingdom, whose civilization came to an end about 2000 B.C. Excavations conducted by Sir Leonard Woolley on the site of ancient Ur have revealed the excellence of its culture and the magnificence of its art. The culture of ancient Sumer anticipated that of Egypt. It had a most notable influence on the later cultures of Babylonia and Assyria, and on the religious pattern of the ancient Near East.

Although it is not possible to establish a precise chronology for Abraham, we are quite sure that the Hebrew patriarch lived in the first half of the second millennium, probably around 1850 B.C. The civilization of Sumer came to an end with the invasion of hordes of Semites from the Syrian steppes. They are called Amorites in the Bible. They dominated the land from the Mediterranean to the Persian Gulf in the period 2000–1700 B.C.[2] Mari, the capital of a state that extended for three hundred miles, was one of the most brilliant cities of the second millennium B.C. It was conquered by Hammurabi about 1700 B.C., under whom the little village of Babylon rose to great renown and a culture surpassing that of Egypt was created. A perennial

[2] Important new knowledge on this phase of history was gained by the excavations at Mari on the Middle Euphrates under the direction of André Parrot. A handsome exhibit of the finds may be seen in the Louvre Museum.

reminder of it stands in the Louvre, the famous Law Code of Hammurabi. A very important aspect of the Babylonian civilization was writing. Cuneiform writing was to influence the civilized world for centuries. It was writing on clay, and is called cuneiform because of the wedge-shaped characters. *Cuneus* is the Latin word for wedge. The language was not alphabetic, but syllabic, an ancient Semitic tongue philologically related to Hebrew.

This was the period of Egyptian history known as the Middle Empire (2000–1780 B.C.), a golden age of culture and a time of great prosperity. Egypt was politically powerful and had control of Syria and Palestine, buffer between the two centers of empire. Petty kingdoms dotted the land bridge over which the Pharaoh exercised a loose kind of control. The Palestine towns of Jerusalem and Sichem are named in Egyptian texts from this period. The social organization of the little kingdoms was patriarchal. They were centered about the hill towns, and between them lay large areas of land, open territory where pastoral tribes might wander at will. One such tribe was the family of Abraham, lately migrated from Haran. The biblical record of Abraham and his descendants is found in Genesis 12–50. The Israelites were the children of Abraham through Jacob, his grandson. Jacob was father to twelve sons who were the ancestors of the twelve tribes that bore their names (eponymous ancestors). The tribe of Juda, for example, descended from Jacob's fourth son Juda. The name Israel is explained by the fact that Jacob's name was changed to Israel as related in Genesis 32:28. Jacob and his sons went down to join Joseph in Egypt, but God assured the patriarch in a vision, "Do not fear to go down to Egypt, for there I will make you a great people" (Gen. 46:3). God had promised Abraham and Jacob that their posterity would possess the land of Canaan.

Abraham and his descendants move in the full light of Near East history in the early second millenium. The same cannot be said for Adam, the original man. The first eleven chapters of Genesis carry the story back beyond Abraham to the origin of man and the origin of the world. From the scientific point of view questions concerning the origin of man and the early phases of the human race do not belong to the domain of history, since history is the record of man's past as known from written records. Such questions pertain to the sciences of physical and cultural anthropology, which interpret man's past from skeletal remains, modes of burial, primitive paintings, and artifacts. This is the period of prehistory. The sciences that investigate the origin of the world are particularly astronomy, geology, and paleontology. An observation is immediately called for. Genesis 1–11 should not be considered a primitive scientific primer on these questions, since it is a religious statement. It is a misdirection therefore to attempt to harmonize its data with the data of modern science. It is religious in character and is to be assessed in terms of theology, not of science. True, the affirmations of the inspired author are expressed in the language of his times.

His imagery in relating the creation of the world and of man is colored by literary forms of the ancient world. The whole section in fact shows signs of marked Mesopotamian influence. For proper interpretation Genesis 1–11 must be read in light of the literatures of ancient Near East, not in terms of books on modern science. This will be discussed more fully in Chapter Four.

There is a great void in the biblical record of Israel's history between the book of Genesis and the book of Exodus. Genesis closes with the death of Joseph in Egypt, and Exodus opens with the career of Moses. Centuries separate these two figures. About these centuries the Bible says not a word. What went on between 1700 and 1200 B.C.? This is the period of Israel's bondage in Egypt, and the events of the period shaped the history in which Israel as a nation was to play an important role.

The entrance of the Semitic tribes of Israel into Egypt is generally related to the conquest of Egypt by the Hyksos about 1700 B.C. Scarabs of the period reveal predominantly Semitic names, pointing to a large Semitic element among the invaders. The invaders conquered by means of a weapon unknown to the Egyptians, the war horse and chariot. They dominated Egypt for more than a century, until driven out about 1570 B.C. The book of Genesis attributes to Joseph an important role in Egyptian affairs. His rise to power is more probable under the rule of Semitic invaders than under native Egyptian princes. The later oppression of Israel is understandable after the return of the native princes to power. The Egyptians were not Semitic but Hamitic, descendants of Noe's son Ham (Cham).

At the other end of the Fertile Crescent in the same period Babylonia likewise reeled before the blows of the invader, and entered a dark age. The assault came from the highlands to the east of the Tigris, first from the Elamites, then from the Kassites. Indo-Iranians and Hurrians from the eastern highlands invaded upper Mesopotamia between 1750 and 1600 B.C. A century later the powerful empire of the non-Semitic Mitanni held the balance of power between the Hittite Empire and Egypt. The Hittites of Asia Minor overpowered the Mitanni about 1370 B.C. and became the dominant power of western Asia, balanced only by a strong Egypt. This period came to a close about 1200 B.C. with the decline of Egyptian and Hittite powers. In Mesopotamia a new power was on the rise, Assyria. Toward the close of the period, before the middle of the thirteenth century, Israel's exodus from Egypt took place, followed by the period of desert wandering. At Mount Sinai the Law was given through Moses and the tribes made a covenant with the Lord. The story of these events and Israel's conquest of Transjordan is told in the books from Exodus to Deuteronomy.

Moses died on the other side of the Jordan after the conquest of the lands beyond the river. The conquest of western Palestine under the leadership of Josue is related in the book of Josue, which also describes the division of the conquered lands among the twelve tribes. Before

1200 B.C. Israel was established in Canaan. The two centuries that followed were a period of consolidation. The land was divided among the twelve tribes and they lived rather separate lives under a form of patriarchal social organization, lovers of freedom and autonomy. They dwelt in the land as conquerors, but were still beset by foes on every side, particularly the Canaanites and Philistines. The latter invaded Canaan about 1190 B.C. They settled along the coastal plain after their expulsion from Egypt which they had attempted to enter. Then began the centuries-long struggle with Israel for the land of Canaan. Tales of this period and exploits of Israel's heroes are told in the book of Judges. This period is also the setting for the book of Ruth.

This brings us to about the year 1000 B.C. Most of our knowledge of the Near East in the second millennium B.C. has come through the science of archeology. Excavations have uncovered the temples, the palaces, the paintings, the pottery, and the plumbing of ancient civilizations; but more important, they have unearthed libraries of countless tablets, especially in cuneiform. These texts have been deciphered to give us worlds of new knowledge, covering practically all aspects of life in biblical times. The texts from the Mari excavations throw light on the Amorite culture that dominated the world of the patriarchs. At Nuzi in northern Mesopotamia texts of the fifteenth century were discovered that reveal legal and social customs akin to the patriarchal customs seen in Genesis. From Ras

Shamra (ancient Ugarit) have come texts that are primary sources on the religion of the Canaanites, erstwhile threat to Israel's faith. The legal code of Hammurabi offers interesting similarities to laws in the code of Sinai. At Tell el-Amarna in Egypt letters have been discovered that proved to be correspondence between the vassals of Palestine and the Egyptian court. They throw light on political conditions in Egypt and Canaan in the fourteenth century B.C.

A most important result of archeological discoveries is the changed picture of the religions of the Near East in the second millennium. Scholars of the last century, such as W. Robertson Smith, drew a picture of these religions as primitive and barbaric. Archeology has discredited that picture. The ancient texts reveal a highly developed and complex religious pattern. Religion was polytheistic, the worship of many gods. It was anthropomorphic; that is, it conceived gods to be like men. The male and female gods personified natural elements. Sin was the moon-god worshipped at Ur. Ra was the sun-god worshipped in Egypt. In Canaan, Baal-Hadad was the god of storm. The gods were thought to dwell in an organized pantheon, which men visualized like the court of the king.

There was a very intimate relationship between the god and the king, going so far in Egypt as to make the king a god. At the head of the heavenly pantheon stood the high god. In the Ugarit pantheon it was El; in Babylon it was Marduk. This pattern prevailed throughout the Near East in the second millennium, but it is marked, particularly in

the second half of the millennium, by a trend toward syncretism. This took two directions: lesser gods were identified with the high god, and the gods of one people were
identified with the gods of other peoples, as later Jupiter
was identified with Zeus. Early in the fourteenth century B.C. in Egypt Amenophis IV attempted to replace all
gods with the one god Aten, personification of the sun.
The attempt was shortlived. The rites of these heathen
religions were marred by such excesses as sacred prostitution connected with the fertility cult and by human
sacrifice. It is against this dark backdrop that the religion
of Abraham, Moses, and the Prophets must be viewed to
understand its significance and its grandeur.

The political situation in the Near East during the last
two centuries of the second millennium has been described
as "a dead calm." Egypt was exhausted from the effort
expended on expelling the Sea Peoples in B.C. 1190 and
continued to decline. The Assyrian empire of Tiglath-
pileser I (c. 1114–1076 B.C.) had a brief burst of life, but
then Assyria had to wait two centuries before another re-
surgence. This was due in part to the pressure of Aramaean
expansion. In Asia Minor the Hittite empire was over-
thrown about 1200 B.C. by an invasion of the Sea Peoples.
The collapse of the great powers gave Palestine time to
work out its own destiny unmolested.

Just before 1000 B.C. a great change took place in Israel's political structure. A monarchy was established with
Saul as the first king (c. 1020 B.C.). The need for a king

was accentuated by the threat of the Philistines, for only by a united front could the Israelite tribes hope for victory. David (c. 1000–960 B.C.) was the second king. He overcame the Philistines and other foes to make Israel the dominant power in Palestine. He made Jerusalem the political and religious capital of the kingdom, and under his son Solomon (c. 960–922 B.C.) it was crowned with the Temple.

The united monarchy did not long endure. Upon the death of Solomon and due in large measure to his policies the ten northern tribes seceded and set up their own kingdom under Jeroboam. They appropriated the name Israel, and set up sanctuaries in Bethel and Dan to rival Jerusalem. The two southern tribes, Juda and Benjamin, formed the kingdom of Juda. The division reduced Israel to two small kingdoms like the neighboring petty states, and by this time the shadow of a giant began to fall over the Near East, again powerful Assyria.

In the middle of the eighth century Syria and Palestine felt the might of Assyria in the campaign of Tiglath-pileser III. Samaria, capital of Israel, fell in 722 B.C. after a long siege, and the people of the northern kingdom were led away into exile, never to return. Notable among the kings of its short history were such colorful figures as Omri, Achab, and Jehu. Remembered among its queens is Jezebel.

The southern kingdom escaped by the skin of its teeth the disaster that befell Israel at the flood tide of Assyrian might. Its survival was God's doing rather than man's. It was not to be Assyria's lot to reduce Juda to shame and defeat. That lot fell to her imperial successor, Chaldea. Assyria suffered a series of defeats at the hands of the Medes and the Chaldeans. Nineveh, the capital, shining symbol of Assyrian might, fell in 612 B.C. In 586 B.C. Nabuchodonosor, the Chaldean, razed Jerusalem after a devastating siege, and the people of Juda were led away into exile, the Babylonian captivity.

The books of Samuel and Kings (1–2 Samuel; 1–2 Kings) tell the story of the united monarchy and the divided kingdom. The book of Chronicles (1–2 Chronicles or Paralipomenon) is a parallel record of sorts with special interest in the dynasty of David, the kingdom of Juda, and its religious institutions. Most of the writing prophets belong to this period, beginning with Amos and Osee (Hosea), prophets of Israel in the eighth century. The prophecies of the great Isaias (1–35) were addressed to the people of Juda in the same century. Micheas (Micah) also belongs to this century. Sophonias, Nahum, and Habacuc prophesied around 600 B.C. Jeremias and Ezechiel preached during the last days of Juda and the Exile. The message of Second-Isaias (40–55) was directed to the exiles, and that of Trito-Isaias (56–66) to the people of Juda after their return from the Exile. To the reign of King David we can trace the beginnings of the Psalter, and to Solomon's reign the origin of maxims and proverbs, whence developed the later Wisdom literature, like the book of Proverbs.

The downfall of the Chaldean empire came quickly. It withered before the hot breath of the indomitable Cyrus. With its demise the long succession of Semitic empires came to end. Persia was Aryan or Indo-Germanic. The Persian empire was to survive for two hundred years as master of the Near East, and its capital Persepolis would surpass the grandeur that was Babylon. Cyrus abandoned the policy of his Assyrian and Chaldean predecessors, who deported conquered peoples. He sent the exiles home. Babylon fell to Cyrus in 539 B.C. and two years later he issued an edict permitting the people of Juda, the Jews, to return to their homeland. The story of the restoration, the rebuilding of Jerusalem's walls and the Temple, are related in the books of Esdras and Nehemias. This is the time of the activity of the two minor prophets Aggeus (Haggai) and Zacharias. The book of Esther may date from the late Persian period, and perhaps the book of Job. The minor prophets Malachias, Joel, Abdias, and Jonas probably belong to the fifth and fourth centuries in the Persian period.

The Persian empire fell with the defeat of Darius in 333 B.C., and the period of Hellenism began. Hellenism takes its name from Hellas, which stood for geographical Greece and Greek settlements everywhere. The conqueror of Darius was Alexander, son of Philip of Macedonia. Alexander was in love with the culture of his land. He could look back on the great cultural tradition of Greece, the heroic epics of Homer, the golden age of Pericles, the wisdom of Plato and Socrates, and an art and architecture without compare. He could look back upon noble traditions of freedom. Perhaps he suspected what we know: that all men are indebted to Greece. Alexander was taught by Aristotle, and nature had endowed him richly. The twenty-year-old conqueror must have appeared superhuman to the peoples of the Near East as he strode like a god over the ancient civilizations. He thought of himself as a god. His dreams went beyond military conquest to embrace the mystical vision that all men must become one. His dream was not fulfilled, but his conquests prepared the world to hear the message of brotherhood from a peaceful Galilean.

Alexander the Great died in Babylon at the age of thirty-three, and his empire was divided among his generals. Egypt fell to Ptolemy, and Syria and the east to Seleucus. Juda found herself between two centers of Hellenism. She was subject to the Ptolemies until 198 B.C. and after that to the Seleucids. Hellenism affected Jews outside of Palestine, but met with resistance within the country. Antiochus IV (175–164 B.C.) of the Seleucid dynasty endeavored to force Hellenism upon the Jews by a vicious persecution of their faith. The Jews rebelled against the Syrian persecutor and succeeded in winning their independence. The record of this heroic fight for freedom is contained in the two books of Machabees. The book of Daniel belongs to this period of Hellenism, as do the books that make up the Wisdom literature, that is, Proverbs, Ecclesiastes, Sirach (Ecclesiasticus), and Wisdom. The books of Judith and Tobias also were written during the Greek period.

Rome succeeded to Greece as imperial master of the world. Palestine became her subject in 63 B.C. At the time Juda was ruled by the descendants of the Machabees, the Hasmonean dynasty. It was misrule rather than rule, marked by family strife over the throne. Herod, the Idumaean, profited from the turmoil to ease his way into power. This was Herod the Great, puppet king of Juda from 37 B.C. to 4 B.C. Near the end of his reign Jesus was born in Bethlehem.[3] Three of Herod's sons succeeded to his kingdom upon his death; two of them were still reigning when Jesus was crucified, Antipas and Philip. The third, Archelaus, had been deposed in A.D. 10 and replaced by a Roman procurator. Pontius Pilate was Procurator in Judea from A.D. 26 to A.D. 36. The year of Jesus' death was probably A.D. 30.

About forty years later the Jewish revolt against Rome broke out. It was crushed by the Roman legions under Vespasian and Titus. After a horrifying siege, Jerusalem and its Temple were reduced to ruins. By this time

[3] Herod died in the year 750 of the Roman era, which corresponds to 4 B.C. Since Jesus was born about two years earlier his birth occurred about six years before the Christian era. This anomaly is due to an error of the sixth century monk, Denis the Little, who wrongly computed the year 754 of the Roman era as A.D. 1.

(A.D. 70) the bulk of the New Testament had been written—the Gospels of Matthew, Mark, and Luke, and the epistles of St. Paul. When the first century came to a close the New Testament was practically complete.

# FOUR

# GENESIS REVISITED

The book of Genesis is not all of a piece. It is a patch-work of many colorful literary bits. Some observations on its literary character may enlighten the reader and spare him a certain perplexity. Let us look first at Genesis 1–11.

Genesis begins with an account of the creation of the world and of Adam, the father of the human race. The story of Abraham, father of the Israelites, begins in Genesis 12. Between Adam and Abraham stands Noe, sur-vivor of the Deluge, described in Genesis 6–9. There is a genealogical table in 11:10–26 that begins with Sem, son of Noe, and closes with Thare (Terah), father of Abraham. By this table Abraham is linked to Noe. There is another genealogy in Genesis 5 that links Noe to Adam. It would seem therefore that the author's intention is to link Abraham, father of Israel, to Adam, father of mankind, and thus place in dramatic relief God's choice of Israel—from all the children of the earth he chose them.

Note further the character of these genealogies. There are ten generations in the table of Genesis 5, ten generations between Adam and Noe. In Genesis 11 there are likewise ten generations, this time between Noe and Thare, father of Abraham. This neat numerical balance puts us on the alert. It suggests that the tables are a literary creation, not an historical record. Note further the rhythmic structure, the repetitious formulae: A lived X years and begot B; A lived after he begot B, Y years; and all the days of A were Z years, and he died. This formula is pronounced ten times in Genesis 5, and a similar formula is repeated a like number of times in Genesis 11. This confirms the impression that we are dealing here with artificial literary structures, fixed patterns. Observe too, the ages of these patriarchs. The age of Adam was 930 years. As the list progresses the ages consistently decrease until Thare, Abraham's father, achieves only 148 years. The nearer we come to historic time, the nearer the ages come to our own. From these brief illustrations of the literary character of the genealogical materials the reader may realize that we encounter here an ancient literary genre and that it would be out of order to consider it an historical record of mankind between Adam and Abraham. Genesis 1–11 contains the remains of comparatively recent traditions.

The genealogies may serve to bring out another point. There are two other genealogical tables in this section, one in Genesis 4, the other in Genesis 10. A comparison of these lists with those we have just considered will reveal notable differences of style. The systematic scheme, the precise ages, the repeated formulae do not appear. These lists are informal and chatty: "Ada bore Jabel: he was forerunner of those who dwell in tents and have flocks. His brother's name was Jubal; he was the forerunner of those who play the harp and the flute" (4:20–22). If we read these lines in the Hebrew text we meet an interesting *jeu des mots*. The name *Yabel* sounds like the verb *yabal* meaning "to lead [flocks]"; the name *Yubal* resembles the word *yobel* which means "trumpet." The ancient Israelite delighted in this word play.

These observations suffice to allow us to point to some implications. These are examples of the literary analysis from which critics derive conclusions as to the literary structures of Genesis. The fact that the book is a composite work made up of various sources is recognized by critics of all schools. Opinion is divided on the number and dates of the sources. Independent critics judge that the genealogies in Genesis 5 and 11 belong to the same source, a document of the fifth century B.C. which is called the Priestly

Document (P). The other two lists, they affirm, belong
to an earlier document, the Yahwist (J) Source of the
ninth century B.C. We shall treat this question of sources
more at length in the following chapter.

Other considerations are now in order that may prove
of greater interest to the average reader. If, as we feel we
have shown, the genealogical tables are literary artifices,
or ancient literary genres, can they be taken as an historical record of man from Adam to Abraham? Can the lon-
gevity of the patriarchs be taken literally? Note well, if the
author created the lists under the influence of the literary forms of his environment, they say no more than he
intended them to say. It is only by a careful study of the
forms that we can hope to discern his intention. In light of
what we have said it is a false step to approach these lists
in search of an historical record of the age of man on earth
or the life span of primitive man. There was no science of
anthropology when Genesis was written. No fossil man
had been uncovered, and the science of paleontology was
yet unborn. The author of Genesis had no scientific knowledge of the age of the earth or the age of man, nor did
God choose to reveal the knowledge to him. His writing
belongs to another category altogether.

The table of nations in Genesis 10 reflects some of the
popular traditions of cultural lore familiar to the author.
The descendants of Ham, Noe's son, are "Chus, Mesraim,
Phut and Canaan" (10:6). These are the names of countries, not persons. Mesraim is the ancient name for Egypt,

still retained in Arabic *Misr*. The table reveals another favorite trait of antiquity: relating a tribe or a nation to the ancestor who gives it its name, the eponymous ancestor. Thus the Kenites (smiths) are said to be descendants of Kain, a smith or forger. *Nomen est omen*.

These random examples show that Genesis cannot be studied in isolation, but must be considered in the context of the literature of the ancient Near East. The motifs in Genesis 1–11 lead us back to Mesopotamia. We find the ancient Babylonian king lists attributing reigns of thousands of years to early kings. The story of the Tower of Babel is undoubtedly associated with the temple towers that dominated cities like Babylon (Babel) and Ur. Perhaps the best illustration of the influence of this environment is the Babylonian narrative of the Flood, which closely resembles the Flood story in Genesis 6–9. The Babylonian account occurs in the epic of Gilgamesh. A copy of it was found on a clay tablet of the seventh century B.C., discovered by George Smith during the excavations at Nineveh in 1872. The Babylonian account was borrowed from the ancient Sumerian story which is preserved in a fragment from Nippur. A cuneiform fragment copied c. 1966 B.C. proves that the West Semitic peoples, the Amorites, had a flood legend as well as the Babylonians and earlier Sumerians.

Utnapishtim was the Babylonian counterpart of Noe. He was directed by one of the gods to build an ark. When the flood came he entered with his family and animals. After the flood he offered a sacrifice to the gods. This very brief outline will serve to show that the general lines of the Genesis story are there. Fuller comparison reveals very notable differences as well. Gods and goddesses are involved in the Babylonian narrative. They become panic-stricken at the disaster they have wrought. They act like frightened children. In Genesis the story is morally motivated. Only one God is involved. The flood is depicted as a punishment for sin. Although the two accounts are similar in details, they are worlds apart in spirit. It is generally recognized that there is no direct literary dependence and also that they reveal environmental affinities.

Relevant data have been supplied by archeology. Evidence of a flood has been found in excavations at Ur and at Kish. It is not surprising that there were floods in Mesopotamia, the very name meaning the land "between the rivers," the Tigris and Euphrates. Archeology, let it be noted, does not supply evidence for a universal flood. When all the relevant data are assembled and weighed, the conclusion would seem to follow that a popular tradition is common to the biblical and Babylonian accounts, and that the inspired author used the popular tradition to teach men a moral lesson. The genre of Genesis 6–9 is therefore didactic rather than historical, and it is bootless to ponder such questions as whether the flood covered the whole earth or destroyed all men. The point of the story is the horror of sin in God's sight.

The first three chapters of Genesis lead us into a more critical area. These chapters are related to questions of

fundamental importance to Christian theology: the creation of the world and of man, the original sin. Nonetheless,
they too must be viewed exegetically in the perspective of
ancient literary forms. When this is done we find that there
are many elements in these chapters that are also found in
pagan myths. The tree of life is a theme of Assyro-Baby-
lonian folklore. The serpent plays a leading role in the
mythologies of the Sumerians, Babylonians, Assyrians,
and Canaanites. In the Babylonian pantheon Ningishzida
is "the serpent god, lord of the earth." In Canaan the serpent
was a symbol of the goddess of fertility, with whose cult
was linked the ritual of sacred prostitution. It is unthinka-
ble in our day to attempt interpretations of Genesis without a consideration of the influence of the ideas and the
imagery of the environment on the inspired book.

We owe our fuller knowledge of the ancient Near East
to the discoveries of archeology. The biblical scholar cannot
in conscience ignore this knowledge. If his interpretations
change and take new directions, it is not an arbitrary whim
or a passion for novelty. Intellectual honesty forces him to
return to the Bible equipped with ever-growing knowledge
of the biblical world. He must confront the fact of mythological details in the first chapters of Genesis. He recognizes
too that Genesis 1–3 is not a polytheistic myth, but a composition dominated by a moral motivation and a monotheis-
tic faith. He is forced to conclude that the inspired author
has used mythological elements with a symbolic meaning
to teach a religious truth. He is forced to make a distinction

between the content of the chapters and their literary form. He sees the literary environment of Genesis influencing the form, as later on Phoenician architecture will influence the Temple of Solomon. He distinguishes what is taught from the way it is taught. In his judgment, to interpret the tree of life as a symbol of immortality involves no implication of denying Adam's grace of immortality; to interpret the serpent as a symbol of the devil is not to exclude the theology of the Fall, but to place it on a sound exegetical foundation.

This distinction between content and form may be perceived more readily in Genesis 1. The six-day frame in which the creative work of God is described is patently modeled on a Jewish work week of six days with Sabbath rest on the seventh. The allotment of God's creative works to various days is a breakdown of the elements of the world according to the author's cosmology; that is, a flat earth floating on seas and a solid vault above. He runs the creation film backwards, as it were, reducing order again to chaos and then shows the film of creation as he imagines it might have happened. This is imaginative writing, albeit divinely inspired. It is not to be confused with revelation or the manifestation of the manner in which God made the world. The revelation in Genesis 1 is that one good principle, God, created all things good; that the sun, moon, and stars are not gods to be served, but elements subject to the one God who alone is to be served. The teaching of Genesis 1 is that God created the world by his omnipotent word. The teaching takes its literary form from the Jewish calendar and the accepted Ptolemaic cosmology.

The text that felt the impact of the theory of evolution was Genesis 2:7: "Then the Lord God formed man out of the dust of the ground." These words seemed to affirm immediate and direct formation of Adam's body by God. There can be no question that this is figurative language. The imagery is that of the potter fashioning a vessel. Like him, God is depicted fashioning man's body. The imagery continues in 2:7, "and [the Lord God] breathed into his nostrils the breath of life and man became a living being." God is depicted as a man. This figure is termed anthropomorphism. The extent of the sacred author's affirmation is rather difficult to determine. From 3:19 ("till you return to the ground, since out of it you were taken; for dust you are and unto dust you shall return") we may conclude that he affirms the origin of man's body from the earth. By the figure of God breathing into his nostrils, we understand that the life principle came directly from God and man's community with God, an idea expressed in 1:26 where man is said to be made "in the image of God." Man's difference from the animals and his lordship over them is another obvious motif of the narrative. The fact that Adam names the animals (2:20) would be an affirmation of his intelligence, since for the Hebrew the name stood for the thing (cf. 2:19).

In light of these considerations we can see the wisdom of the words of Pope Pius xii in *Humani Generis* (August

12, 1950). "Accordingly, the Magisterium of the Church does not forbid that the theory of evolution concerning the origin of the human body as coming from pre-existent and living matter—for Catholic faith obliges us to hold that the human soul is immediately created by God—be investigated and discussed by experts as far as the present state of human sciences and sacred theology allow."

We must bring these remarks on Genesis 1–11 to a close. They are presented by way of guidance to the reader, as suggestive rather than final regarding the interpretation of these chapters. The Biblical Commission in its letter to Cardinal Suhard in January 1948 stated, "The question of the literary forms of the first eleven chapters of Genesis is far more obscure and complex. These literary forms do not correspond to any of our classical categories and cannot be judged in the light of the Greco-Roman or modern literary types. . . . If it is agreed not to see in these chapters history in the classical and modern sense, it must be admitted also that known scientific facts do not allow a positive solution of all the problems which they present. . . . To declare *a priori* that these narratives do not contain history in the modern sense of the word might easily be understood to mean that they do not contain history in any sense, whereas, they relate in simple and figurative language, adapted to the understanding of mankind at a lower stage of development, the fundamental truths underlying the divine scheme of salvation, as well as a popular description of the origins of the human race and of the chosen people."

Genesis 12–50 must be classified in a different category from the first eleven chapters. This part of the book opens with Abraham and tells of the forefathers of Israel down to Joseph. Since Abraham lived in the first half of the second millennium he belongs to the historical period, a period well documented by written records. We do not mean to infer by this that the patriarchal narratives in Genesis belong to a strictly historical genre. History writing in the strict sense came later, when Israel was constituted as a nation. Hebrew tradition does not ascribe written records to Abraham, but to Moses. It is fairly certain that the patriarchal narratives for the most part derive from oral traditions. Let it be noted at once that oral traditions of antiquity are not a thing to be spurned. Among the nomads oral traditions substituted for written records, and the reliability of transmission was assured by the incredible memories of the orientals. There are reports of Jews who knew the Bible by heart, and even the Talmud.

The patriarchal narratives recently received striking corroboration from discoveries made at Nuzi in northern Mesopotamia. Thousands of clay tablets were found, written by Hurrian scribes in the fifteenth century B.C. They reveal customs and laws that parallel those of the patriarchs; for example, the legal customs surrounding the relation of Abraham to his concubine Agar (Gen. 16). The discoveries at Mari lent their confirmation of the reliability of the Genesis onomasticon, or list of names. Place names in the Mari documents confirm the authenticity of biblical names like Haran and Nachor. These and other archeological finds have demonstrated that many reliable historical data are preserved in Israel's traditions about her forefathers.

This must not be taken to mean that we are to place Genesis 12–50 in the same category as, let us say, Caesar's Gallic Wars. Certain observations on its literary characteristics will discourage that. In Genesis 17:17 we read that Abraham was a hundred years old when Isaac was born and Sara was ninety. From 12:4 we learn that they migrated to Canaan twenty-five years before. At that time Sara would have been sixty-five. It is somewhat disconcerting therefore to read in 12:14 that "the Egyptians saw that the woman was very beautiful." This inconsistency is best explained by admitting the existence of different documents in Genesis that are conflated into one composition without adjustment of details. What strikes the contemporary reader as unusual is that these inconsistencies did not seem to bother the later compiler. This phenomenon is not restricted to Genesis. It occurs throughout the Pentateuch and in the later historical books as well. We meet it even in the medieval Arabic chroniclers.

Sara's beauty is the reason for her abduction by the Pharaoh of Egypt after Abraham had declared that she was his sister. Abraham fares well because of Sara, but not so the Pharaoh. He is visited with plagues, after which

it is realized she is Abraham's wife and she is returned
(12:10–20). A similar story is related in Genesis 20. This
time the place is Gerara and the king is Abimelech. Abraham again declares, "She is my sister." In this chapter
greater ethical concern is expressed, for we are assured that
God did not allow Abimelech to touch her and Abraham
explains that she is indeed his sister, "my father's daughter,
but not my mother's" (20:12). The moral tone is higher.
The same motif is found in the life of Isaac (26:6–11).
The impression is created that in the three instances we
are dealing with the one basic motif, which appears in the
oral traditions with certain modifications. The motivation
of the inspired author in using this tradition seems to be
to show God's particular care for Abraham and Isaac.

Such excursions in literary criticism interest the Bible
reader less than questions about the ethical standards of
Abraham and the patriarchs. Abraham says of his wife,
"She is my sister," and saves his skin by allowing her to
be taken into the palace of Pharaoh. It does seem a rather
cavalier handling of a wife and of the truth. This is not
an isolated instance of what appears to the Christian conscience as low-grade ethics. The brazen example is Jacob's
outright lie to his father Isaac in Genesis 27. It seems to
us pointless to try to explain away this conduct by an
exercise of casuistic legerdemain. The fact is that the biblical authors put these things down. They do not endorse
them or hold them up for imitation. We have shown above
that the patriarchal narratives are early traditions handed

down by oral transmission over centuries. They have the authentic flavor of the Bedouin camp, the outlook of the wandering tribesmen, the odor of the tent and the fire. And that is precisely what the Bible says the patriarchs were: wandering Aramaeans.

The biblical record does not make them out to be angels, but men—men who despite their ignorance and their weakness responded to the touch of God. Divine revelation begins with Abraham, it does not end with him. There is a forward march of the truth of God; the first steps of that march were taken by Abraham. He was called from a pagan family of moon-worshippers (cf. Josue 24:2)[1] to serve the true God, to become a pilgrim in a land he knew not. In response to the mystical call he came to the land of Canaan. This became the Land of Promise, promised to a mighty people that would come from Abraham. In Abraham, man of faith, the ascent of conscience began. It would continue to climb until it rested at the peak that is Christ.

The figure of Abraham had great significance for St. Paul. The faith of Abraham was used as a telling argument in his epistles to the Galatians and the Romans. The story of Sara and Agar was interpreted "allegorically" in Galatians. Excerpts from the life of Abraham are read in the pre-Lenten Office beginning on Quinquagesima Sunday. In Isaac carrying the wood for the sacrificial fire, the

[1] Cf. Judith 5:7–9. Abraham's native city, Ur, was a center of the cult of the moon-god, Sin.

Church beholds an Old Testament type of Christ carrying the cross. Following St. Paul, the Church sees in Abraham the father of them that believe. "The men of faith are the real sons of Abraham" (Gal. 3:7). His name is spoken in every Mass, and he is called "our father Abraham."

# FIVE

# THE BIRTH OF THE NATION

The patriarchs were Israel's forebears, and their story is
the prehistory of the nation. Jacob's name was changed to
Israel (*isr-el*, he who contends with God). He was the
eponymous ancestor of the tribes. The history of the nation
begins with the book of Exodus. Here we meet Moses,
father of the nation under God. The scene of the opening
act of the drama is the Nile Delta. The time is the early
thirteenth century, when the tribes felt the heavy hand of
the oppressor in Rameses II (c. 1301–1234 B.C.) of the
XIX Dynasty.

The exodus of Israel from Egypt and the events surrounding it, the plagues and the crossing of the Red Sea, are immortalized in the Old Testament. They were remembered not only in the historical accounts of Israel's past, but in her poetry and prophecy. The national literature would not let the people forget that the Lord proved himself in Egypt. He entered into history and proved himself mightier than the armies of Pharaoh, mightier than the gods of Egypt. The book of Exodus describes the *mirabilia Dei,* the wondrous works of God. This theme that resounds throughout the Old Testament is first sounded here.

The most wondrous work of all was God's choice of Israel to be his very own people. The Deuteronomist could ask, "Did any god venture to go and take a nation for himself from the midst of another nation, by testings, by signs and wonders, by war, with his strong hand and outstretched arm, and by great terrors, all of which the Lord, your God, did for you in Egypt before your very eyes?" (Deut. 4:34). The Lord led Israel out of Egypt "personally" (4:37). This was a kindness Israel's spiritual leaders never forgot, the mystery of divine election. It is a concept central to the understanding of the Old Testament.

The events of the Exodus begot more than a literary monument, a memorial of words. They begot a memorial of rites as well. Israel's greatest feast, the Pasch or Passover, was a memorial of the flight from Egypt and the death of Egypt's firstborn. The Passover is called today the

Seder, that is, order or rite. Unto this day the first question at the Seder service, asked by the youngest present, is "Why does this night differ from all nights of the year?" More than three thousand years after the event the memorial rite lives on. The book of Exodus prescribes, "You shall observe this as a perpetual ordinance for yourselves and your descendants. . . . When your children ask you 'What does this rite mean?' you shall reply, 'This is the Passover sacrifice of the Lord, who passed over the houses of the Israelites in Egypt; when he struck down the Egyptians he spared our houses'" (12:24–27).

More meaningful to the Christian are his own memorial rites in which the themes of Exodus and Pasch live on in fulfillment. The Christian liturgy is heir to the spiritual treasures of the New Testament and the Fathers of the Church. St. Paul declared that "Christ, our passover, has been sacrificed" (1 Cor. 5:7). As the Israelites were saved by the blood of the lamb sprinkled on their doorposts, we are saved by the blood of "the lamb of God, who takes away the sin of the world" (John 1:29). The unleavened bread of the Eucharist is a perpetual reminder that Jesus instituted the Sacrifice and the Sacrament of our altar at a Paschal Supper. New Testament scholars note a strong influence of the Jewish liturgy on the formation of the Gospels, particularly John. It is an attractive suggestion that the structure of the Fourth Gospel is related to the Jewish cycle of feasts, notably three passover feasts. In imitation of the New Testament writers the Fathers saw in the events of the Exodus types of Christian realities. The crossing of the Red Sea is a type of redemption, the blood of the lamb is a type of the redeeming blood of Christ. This typology pervades the Church liturgy and reaches its most dramatic expression in the liturgy of Holy Week.

The Lord led Israel out of Egypt with signs and wonders, but even greater things awaited them at Mount Sinai. There the covenant was wrought between Yahweh and Israel. When the people were still in Egypt, Yahweh had promised, "I will take you as my own people, and you shall have me as your God" (Ex. 6:7). At Sinai the promise was fulfilled. The power and majesty of Yahweh were manifested in the desert wilderness where the red peaks of Sinai reared. "Mount Sinai was all wrapped in smoke, for the Lord came down upon it in fire. The smoke rose from it as from a furnace, and the whole mountain trembled violently. The trumpet blast grew louder and louder, while Moses was speaking and God answering him in thunder" (19:18 f.). There Israel received the Ten Commandments and the Law. There the covenant was ratified in blood. "Taking the Book of the Covenant, he read it aloud to the people, who answered, 'All that the Lord has said, we will heed and do.' Then he took the blood and sprinkled it on the people saying, 'This is the blood of the covenant which the Lord has made with you in accordance with all these words of his'" (Ex. 24:7 f.). By virtue of the covenant

Israel was sworn to the Lord and Lord to Israel. The covenant idea is fundamental in the religion of Israel.

Exodus associates the revelation of the name Yahweh with the events at Mount Sinai (3:13 ff.). This was given to Moses as the proper name of God. Since the earlier Hebrew manuscripts were consonantal texts, that is, written without vowels, the pronunciation was unknown until relatively recent times. Four consonants form the name: YHWH. In later Judaism it was never uttered, out of a sense of respect. The form Jehovah arose as a result of misunderstanding on the part of early translators. Since the Jews did not pronounce the name, the vowels of a substitute word were placed in their Bibles about the four consonants. Not realizing this the translators read it as it stood, thus begetting the hybrid form. The original meaning of the name is not certain. It is commonly explained as defining God as absolute and necessary Being. Professor Albright has suggested that Yahweh is the remnant of an originally longer formula meaning "He causes to be what is." The Bible of Jerusalem favors the interpretation of 3:14 as "I am what I am," that is, I cannot be named or defined. In the third person Yahweh, "He is," would mean to the Israelite the God who had shown himself faithful and powerful in the deeds of deliverance.

Centuries later in times of Israel's infidelity her prophets would look back longingly upon this trysting time. How tenderly Osee recalls it, "Saith the Lord . . . 'Behold, I will allure her, and will lead her into the wilderness, and

I will speak to her heart . . . and she shall sing there according to the days of her youth, and according to the days of her coming up out of the land of Egypt'" (2:13 ff.).

From what has been said the reader will note that the book of Exodus describes rites and laws as well as events. We find in it the creed, the code, and the cult of early Israel. The same is true of the other books of the Pentateuch, which is called the Law (Torah) by the Jews. A careful reading of these books will create certain questions in the reader's mind. In the matter of laws, for example, certain differences may be observed in the two forms of the Decalogue, in Exodus 20:1–17 and in Deuteronomy 5:6–21. Let us compare the commandment of Sabbath rest in both forms.

| | |
|---|---|
| Remember to keep holy the Sabbath day. | Take care to keep holy the Sabbath day as the Lord, your God, commanded you. |
| Six days you may labor and do all your work but the seventh day is the Sabbath of the Lord your God. | Six days you may labor and do all your work but the seventh day is the Sabbath of the Lord your God. |
| No work may be done, either by you,<br>or your son or daughter,<br>or your male or female slave,<br>or your beast,<br>or by the alien that lives with you. | No work may be done, either by you,<br>or your son or daughter,<br>or your male or female slave,<br>or your ox or ass, or any of your beasts,<br>or the alien who lives with you. |

| | |
|---|---|
| In six days the Lord made the heavens and the earth and all that is in them, but on the seventh day he rested. | Your male and female slave should rest as you do. <br> For remember that you too were once slaves in Egypt. <br> And the Lord your God brought you out from there with his strong hand and outstretched arm. |
| That is why the Lord God has blessed the seventh day and made it holy. | That is why the Lord, your God, has commanded you to observe the Sabbath. |

The motive appealed to by the Deuteronomist is Israel's remembrance of her own slavery in Egypt. This humanitarian motivation is characteristic of the Deuteronomist tradition (cf. 14:26 f.). The motive in Exodus is transcendental, reminiscent of the Creation account in Genesis 1. Both Genesis 1 and the Exodus Decalogue are assigned to the Priestly recension by independent critics. The motivation given in Exodus is considered a later elaboration of the original commandment, which was probably brief in form like the fifth commandment, "Thou shalt not kill." The motive of Sabbath observance given by Deuteronomy would also be a later elaboration.

Another illustration of this kind may prove interesting. Compare the prescriptions for the Passover as given in Exodus (12:1–20) and Deuteronomy (16:1–8). The comparison reveals an emphasis in Deuteronomy that is not found in Exodus. The former speaks of "families" and "household," and prescribes that the blood of the lamb "mark the houses where you are." The latter prescribes that the Passover sacrifice be offered "in the place where he chooses as the dwelling place of his name" (16:2). Israel is warned, "You may not sacrifice the Passover in any of the communities which the Lord, your God, gives; only at the place which he chooses as the dwelling place of his name. . . . You shall cook and eat it at the place the Lord, your God, chooses" (16:5 ff.). The emphasis on "the place" is noteworthy. "The place" is the Temple of Jerusalem. Centralization of worship was characteristic of the reform of King Josias in 621 B.C.

To what purpose do we make these observations? To point out that the laws of the Pentateuch reveal a development. Is this surprising? It would be surprising if they did not, for it is of the nature of law to undergo revision and adaptation to changing conditions. The Biblical Commission affirms this explicitly in the letter to Cardinal Suhard, "No one today . . . rejects a gradual increase of Mosaic laws due to the social and religious conditions of later times." Our purpose has been to demonstrate that the Pentateuch is a work of composite character. This literary aspect of the work will make itself felt even to the casual reader. We chose to illustrate the point by laws, wherein the development is more easily observed and more readily understood. The same fact, however, is observable in the historical sections of the Pentateuch. Therefore the Biblical Commission's letter just quoted declares that the same process of development is "manifest also in the historical narratives." Careful study of the historical sections of the Pentateuch reveal that the history of Israel was rewritten for spiritual edification and religious inspiration. Cult and ritual also exercised an influence on the form that the history finally took. Consequently it would be a mistake to look upon history in the Pentateuch as historical writing that conforms to norms of critical method in the modern sense. The history in Exodus is perhaps best described as an epic.

The story of Israel's wandering in the desert of Sinai, begun in Exodus, is continued in the book of Numbers. It is so called because it contains records of two censuses taken in the course of the desert years (Chapters 1; 26). Like Exodus, Numbers is a combination of law and history. The third book of the Pentateuch, Leviticus, is named from the tribe of Levi, the tribe dedicated to divine service. It is almost entirely legal in character, consisting of sacrificial and other ritual laws prescribed for the Levitical priesthood. Deuteronomy, the last book of the Pentateuch, is so named because the Greeks looked upon it as "second law" or repetition of the Law. Actually it is more than that, being an expansion of the earlier law. The book presents a series of discourses ascribed to Moses. The events described cover the last days of Moses. The book closes with his death.

The Torah of the Jews, the five scrolls or Pentateuch

of the Greeks, was called "the five books of Moses" by the Latins. The tradition was universal among all three that it was the work of the great lawgiver of Israel, Moses. His position and prestige in post-exilic Judaism were unparalleled. According to the Talmud the Torah enjoyed a special grade of inspiration, greater than the other Scriptures. The teaching of the Torah was a touchstone to test the inspiration of later books. In the time of Jesus the Torah of Moses dominated Judaism. It was the supreme religious authority regulating their whole lives. The Christian placed Christ above Moses, but the lawgiver of Israel continued to hold an eminent place in his esteem. His place was high in the ranks of the great men of old, through whom God had spoken. A monument to the Christian feeling for Moses may be seen in the Moses of Michelangelo, whose hands were the hands of the Christian Renaissance and whose heart expressed its spirit.

The Jewish and Christian tradition of Mosaic authorship of the Torah was universally accepted until the nineteenth century, when the science of literary criticism was applied to the Bible. Criticism cannot dwarf the heroic figure of Moses. It can throw light on the literary character of the "five books of Moses." The history of the development of Pentateuchal criticism cannot be repeated here, but its conclusions can be briefly described. The synthesis associated with the name Julius Wellhausen (+1918) is called the Four Source theory on the literary character of the Pentateuch. According to the theory the ancient traditions of Israel were preserved in the northern and southern kingdoms after the division of the monarchy in 922 B.C. From these traditions two literary works arose, the first in the southern kingdom of Juda about 850 B.C., the second in Israel about 750 B.C. Because it preferred the divine name Yahweh the former was called the Yahwist Document (J, because of the German spelling *Jahweh*); the latter was called the Elohist Document (E) because it preferred the name Elohim for God. The third component part was said to be Deuteronomy (D), written about 630 B.C. The fourth and final part was called the Priestly Code (P), the heart of which is Leviticus 17–26. This document was dated after the Exile, about 450 B.C.

The dates assigned to the four sources or documents show that the theory divorced the Torah from Moses. As originally presented by Wellhausen, the literary analysis was part of a synthesis of Israelite history that labored under the method of historical determinism and an evolutionary philosophy. Old Testament research since Wellhausen's time has completely discredited his thesis as such. This change is due primarily to the science of archeology, through which we possess reliable information about the peoples of the ancient Near East, their literatures, and their religions. In light of this new knowledge the aprioristic positions of Wellhausen could not stand.

In the second place the collapse of classical Wellhausenism is due to critical studies of the Old Testament along lines other than source analysis, namely, the study of individual literary forms in the effort to fix their original historical setting. This study, together with research in the nature and function of oral traditions, has been identified with the Scandinavian scholars particularly. The result of these researches was the recognition of much older materials in the Pentateuch than supposed by the Wellhausen school. The best critical scholarship today recognizes the existence of authentic old traditions in the Pentateuch.

The reaction of the Catholic Church to the Wellhausen theory was unfavorable. This was due to two causes particularly: first, the complete disregard for the centuries-old Jewish and Christian tradition on Mosaic authorship; and secondly, the philosophic orientation of the theory, an evolutionary philosophy which the Church could not endorse. The practical outcome of this was the publication of a number of directives by the Biblical Commission to the effect that substantially (*quoad substantiam*) Moses was the author of the Pentateuch. Non-Catholic critics found this action very disturbing and responded with notable agitation. The decrees were published in June 1906. In 1938 Professor Coppens of the University of Louvain published a series of articles in the *Nouvelle Revue Théologique* in which he reviewed questions of Old Testament criticism, among them the Pentateuch question. The articles later appeared in book form and in English translation under the title *The Old Testament and the Critics*. The book is significant since it marks a change of direction in the Catholic attitude toward the question in hand. Professor Coppens suggested a broader interpretation of the decrees on Mosaic authorship of the Pentateuch.

It may be noted here that the infallible teaching authority of the Church is not involved in decrees of the Biblical Commission. They are directives of a very serious nature it is true, but conditioned by the times in which they appear. They do admit of later revision and modification, if in the judgment of the Commission the case demands it. In January 1948 the Biblical Commission replied to two questions proposed to it by the late Cardinal Suhard, Archbishop of Paris, concerning the sources of the Pentateuch and the historicity of the first eleven chapters of Genesis. In reply to the first question the Commission referred to recent historical and critical studies and concluded, "We invite Catholic scholars to study these problems with an open mind in light of sane criticism and of the results of other sciences which have their part in these matters, and such study will without doubt establish the large share and the profound influence of Moses as author and legislator."

Today the progressive wing of Catholic scholars accepts the critical position on the literary composition of the Pentateuch in its basic form, that is, the existence of four

sources of different dates incorporating much older ma-
terial. This is the position taken by the modern French
Bible published under the direction of the Dominican
Fathers of the École Biblique in Jerusalem, familiarly
called the Bible of Jerusalem. The introduction to the
Pentateuch states that it is composed of four "traditions."
These are substantially the same as the documents of the
Four Source theory with the dates assigned them. The
part of Moses is thus described: "The religion of Moses
marked forever the faith and practice of the people. The
Law of Moses remained its norm. Adaptations demanded
by changing times were made in his spirit and vested with
his authority." This describes the position of many Catholic scholars today.

The book of Josue is so named, not because Josue is the
author, but because he is the central character. At the end
of Deuteronomy, Josue was appointed successor to Moses,
and the book of Josue takes up the story where Deuteronomy leaves off. The first part of the book (1–12) relates
the conquest of the Promised Land. The second part (13–
21) describes the division of the land among the tribes.
The final section (22–24) narrates the end of Josue's
career and his last address to the people at Sichem. We
may say that the land of Canaan is the central subject of
the book. The tribes that became the people of Yahweh
in the Sinai desert now receive the land from his hands.
It is Yahweh who fights their battles, Yahweh who is vic-

torious, Yahweh who gives them the inheritance promised to their forefathers, the patriarchs of old (cf. 23:3, 5).

Critical study of the book of Josue reveals the complex character of the literary materials, ancient traditions at the core worked over by a series of editings. The intricate problem of reconstructing the history in detail need not occupy the average Bible reader. It suffices that he know that the history has been idealized and simplified. The epic of the Exodus is continued and becomes an epic of the Conquest, in which the Lord miraculously intervenes on behalf of his people. History is simplified in the sense that events are centered around the personality of Josue, whereas in fact the conquest and division of the land was a longer and more complicated process. The chronology cannot be reconstructed with precision, but it is probable that Israel was installed in Canaan by 1225 B.C.

After the installation in Canaan, Israel was a loose confederation of tribes united by the bond of religion, by the covenant with Yahweh. The renewal of the covenant at Sichem was therefore of great significance. The people replied to Josue, "We will still serve the Lord [Yahweh]" (24:21). This was the force that would hold the tribes together until political unity came with the monarchy.

The book of Josue is religious history. Its purpose is didactic. In its present form it reveals the editorial hand of a school of pious men who draw a religious lesson from Israel's past. According to recent scholarship this is the Deuteronomist school, to which are attributed one or more editings of the history of Israel from Josue to Kings. The school did not destroy the original character of the oral traditions and written documents. As a result critics feel that these forms can be studied for historical evidence on the early history of Israel in Canaan. This technical aspect of Old Testament studies need not engage the common reader, but he may be interested in knowing about it.

The significance of the book is in its religious message. In Chapter 23 Josue is reported as saying to the people, "So now acknowledge with your whole heart and soul that not one of all the promises the Lord, your God, made to you has remained unfulfilled. Every promise has been fulfilled for you, with not one single exception" (23:14). The purpose of the book is to demonstrate the Lord's fidelity to his promises in the conquest of the land promised to the forefathers. The lesson of the book is that fidelity demands fidelity. "If you transgress the covenant of the Lord, your God, which he enjoined on you, serve other gods and worship them, the anger of the Lord will flare up against you and you will quickly perish from the good land which he has given you" (23:16).

The book of Judges might more accurately be called the book of heroes. It tells of the *shophetim*, who were not judges in the sense of magistrates, but in the sense of military leaders. They were leaders of the tribes in time of trouble. Ordinarily a judge had to do only with one tribe or another; occasionally with several, as in the cases of Gideon and Debora and Barac. The judges have this in common, that each of them received from God the charismatic grace of leadership, especially in time of battle against Israel's enemies. The enemies of Israel were the Canaanites who lived in their midst, neighboring peoples like the Moabites, Ammonites, Madianites, and the Philistines. The time indications of the book do not permit us to work out a precise chronology. They are for the most part quite artificial. The frequently occurring number 40 probably is symbolic. Then, too, we must remember that since not all the tribes were engaged, the actions related could have been synchronous. At all events it seems that these exploits in Israel's history must be placed between 1150 and 1000 B.C.

Recent critical study has shown that many ancient traditions are preserved in the book. They throw light on the social and religious conditions in early Israel. Not all the stories need be taken as literal history. Some of them obviously belong to the genre of sagas or legends. The editorial hand of the Deuteronomist school is evident in the book. It is the religious theme of the school that gives the book its unity and its didactic value. The theme is expressed frequently. "Because they had thus abandoned him [Yahweh] and served Baal and the Astharthes, the anger of the Lord flared up against Israel and he delivered them over to plunderers who despoiled them. . . . Even when the Lord raised up judges to deliver them from the power of their despoilers, they did not listen to their judges, but abandoned themselves to the worship of other gods. . . . Whenever the Lord raised up judges for them, he would be with the judge and save them from the power of their enemies as long as the judge lived; . . . But when the judge died, they would lapse and do worse than their fathers, following other gods in service and worship" (2:13–19).

The charming story of Ruth belongs to the period of Judges, although the book in its present form is of much later date. The purpose of the story is beautifully expressed by Booz: "May you receive a full reward from the Lord, God of Israel, under whose wings you have come for refuge" (2:12). The exquisite lesson of the book is that the mercy of the Lord extends to the stranger from Moab. The book has a Davidic connotation. Ruth, the Moabitess, begot Obed, who was father to the father of David the king.

# SIX

# AN ARRAY OF KINGS AND PROPHETS

Samuel was the last of the Judges, a prophetic figure rather than a warrior. The next two books of the Bible bear his name, 1–2 Samuel. The original Hebrew work was just one book. The division was made by the Greek translators, who joined it with 1–2 Kings, also originally one, under the title 1–4 Kings. The Vulgate follows the Greek Old Testament, and the Douay imitates the Vulgate.

Samuel is the subject of the book, not its author. His story opens at Shiloh, the central sanctuary of the Israelite tribes, and seat of the ark of the covenant. The sanctuary at Shiloh was the heart of Yahwism and symbol of the faith that bound the tribes together in a theocracy with Yahweh as king. In the effort to turn the Philistine tide, the tribes bore the ark of the covenant into battle, as an infallible talisman of victory. Despite it they were routed disastrously and the ark fell into the hands of the Philistines (1 Sam. 4). Now the solitary and empty sanctuary of Shiloh was a symbol of Israel's need for a rallying point around which they might unite against the Philistines. Then the cry for a king went up, a king "as all the nations have" (1 Sam. 8:5), and the Israelite monarchy was born.

It is important to note that Israel did not abandon the theocratic ideal with the institution of the monarchy. "The Hebrew king was a charismatic leader, an instrument through which the Lord worked, and as such he possessed a sacred character; he was 'the anointed of the Lord.' But he could not rise above the subjection to the Lord which was the proper position of every human being. Not the will of the king, but the will of the Lord was the supreme law of the land."[1] Kingship was more than a political institution for Israel. It would come to be looked on as the framework in which the will of the Lord would achieve its final realization.

Saul was the first king of Israel (c. 1020–1000 B.C.). The charismatic character of his kingship is manifested in his anointing by Samuel (1 Sam. 10:1). The anointing

[1] J. L. McKenzie, *The Two-edged Sword*, p. 140.

was a sign of the divine choice, and Saul's later failure is interpreted as a rejection by the Lord. The monarchy achieved political and religious prestige with Saul's successor David (c. 1000–960 B.C.). The history of King David begins in 1 Samuel 16 and continues to the beginning of 1 Kings. This part of the record, beginning at 2 Samuel 9, is, in the judgment of critics, the work of an eyewitness and dates from the early years of Solomon's reign. It demonstrates Israel's recognized genius for writing history.

David's military prowess was demonstrated by his victories over the Philistines, his clearing out of Canaanite pockets like Jerusalem, his defeat of neighboring peoples like the Moabites. David's political skill was demonstrated by his choice of the newly won Jerusalem as capital, lying as it did in territory neutral to northern and southern tribes. He made it the national sanctuary with the transfer there of the ark, which had been housed at Kiriath-jearim since its recovery from the Philistines.

The real significance of David in the history of Israel emerges from the Davidic covenant described in 2 Samuel 7:8, 11–16. This is an oracle of Yahweh through the prophet Nathan in response to David's desire to build a house [temple] for Yahweh. (Emphasis supplied.)

Thus says Yahweh of hosts:

. . . . . . . . . . . . . . . . . .
> Yahweh will make a house of you,
> When your days are completed
> and you sleep with your fathers,

*I will raise up for you descendants after you,*
*the offspring of your body,*
and *I will make firm his kingship.*
It is he who shall build a house for my name,
and *I will make firm forever the throne of his kingship.*
*I will be a father to him,*
*and he a son to me;*
If he acts wickedly I will chastise him
with the rod men use,
with blows the sons of men give.
*But my covenant-love shall not be taken from him,*
as I took it from his predecessor:
*Your house and your kingship shall endure forever before*
*me,*
*Your throne is set firm forever.*

This oath of Yahweh expresses a new development in
the covenant idea. At Sinai the covenant was ratified between Yahweh and the nation. Here the covenant is between Yahweh and Davidic kings, not as individuals but
as incorporating the nation and responsible for its welfare.
In Exodus 4:22 the Lord says, "Israel is my son, my firstborn." In 2 Samuel 7:14 the Lord says of the Davidic
dynasty "I will be a father to him, and he a son to me."
As the nation stood in relation to Yahweh as adoptive son,
now the Davidic kings shall be his adopted sons. This is
not a rejection of the former covenant, for the union of the
people with God now takes the form of monarchy. The

people will endure eternally in their relationship with the Lord, because an eternal dynasty is promised.

By virtue of the oracle the destiny of Israel became inseparable from the destiny of the Davidic dynasty. The dynasty became the vehicle of the covenant between Yahweh and Israel. The nation's hope of God's saving intervention in history is bound up with the "anointed" kings of David's line. For this reason this phase is described as royal Messianism. Second Samuel 7 is considered the fundamental text of royal Messianism. Its theme is echoed in Psalm 88 (89):27 ff.

> He [David] shall say of me, You are my father,
>   my God, the Rock, my savior.
> And I will make him the first-born,
>   highest of the kings of the earth,
> Forever I will maintain my kindness toward him,
>   and my covenant with him stands firm.
> I will make his posterity endure forever,
>   and his throne as the days of heaven.

Its echo is heard in the lines of Psalm 2:6 f.

>       (The Lord speaks.)
>     I myself have set up my king
>     on Sion, my holy mountain.
>       (The king speaks.)
> I will proclaim the decree of the Lord:
> The Lord said to me, You are my son;
>   This day I have begotten you. . . .

This theme will grow and grow in prophecies and psalms until one day in Jerusalem the crowds will cry out, saying,

Hosanna to the Son of David!
Blessed is he who comes in the name of the Lord,

And Matthew will write that this was done in fulfillment of that which was spoken by the prophet (21:5 ff., cf. Zach. 9:9).

Tell the daughter of Sion:
Behold, thy king comes to thee,
Meek and seated upon an ass. . . .

It fell to Solomon, David's son, to build the house of the Lord in Jerusalem. King Solomon reigned from 960 to c. 922 B.C. and the history of his reign is told in 1 Kings 1–11. The king turned to Hiram of Tyre for the materials and the technical skills that were not to be found in Israel. The site of the Temple was the threshing floor of Araunah, to the north of the old city. The Temple itself, as opposed to the sacred precinct, was small, being about a hundred feet long and thirty wide. The gemlike structure of white limestone faced the east. In front of it under the open sky stood the massive natural rock that served as the altar of burnt offerings. This is very likely the stone that is now housed by that exquisite piece of Moslem art, the Dome of the Rock. The architecture of Solomon's Temple was Syro-Palestinian, as might be surmised from the artisans employed, those of Tyre. A temple excavated at Tell Tainat gives the best analogy to it.

The Temple itself was not intended for worshipers who remained in the courts without. Only the priests entered the Temple, and only one priest, the high priest, entered into its most sacred inner chamber once a year on the Day of Atonement (Yom Kippur). This inmost room was called the Holy of Holies (*Debir*). It was a windowless room, a perfect cube in shape. In the darkness stood the most sacred cult object of Israel, the ark of the covenant. Above it hovered two figures fifteen feet high, the guardian Cherubim. Here Yahweh was believed to dwell in invisible presence.

Jerusalem now had received its crown, its glory. Now the songs of Sion could be born. The psalmist could cry:

> His foundation upon the holy mountains
> The Lord loves. . . . (86 [87]:1)

and in his burning ardor could sing:

> How lovely is your dwelling place,
> O Lord of hosts! (83 [84] :2)

And when it was no more, men would lament and say:

> Is this the city of perfect beauty,
> the joy of all the earth?
> (Lam. 2:15)

Solomon's reign was marked by extensive building and expansive trade. Excavations directed by Nelson Glueck at Ezion-geber (Elath) have revealed it to be the Pittsburgh of the tenth century B.C. Iron and copper were refined in the smelting furnaces that are the largest and most complex recovered from antiquity. This was the port of Solomon's fleet as well. His court in Jerusalem took on the opulence and luxury characteristic of oriental kings. The taxes and levies needed to support that way of life built up resentment and tension among the people, and ultimately led to the breakup of David's hard-won unity. After the death of Solomon in 922 B.C. the northern tribes seceded and the work of David was undone. The ten northern tribes kept the name Israel, and the southern tribes of Benjamin and Juda were called the kingdom of Juda.

The northern tribes set up a rival king in Jeroboam (c. 922–901 B.C.), who set up rival sanctuaries to Jerusalem at Bethel and Dan. He had golden calves erected at the shrines, not as idols to be worshiped but as symbols or thrones of Yahweh's invisible presence. To the people, prone to idol worship, they were an inevitable occasion of idolatry. Soon Bethel and Dan were centers of worship of the golden calf.

The kingdom of Israel survived for two centuries of hurly-burly and blood-letting. Dynasty succeeded dynasty at the edge of the sword. The cast of kings lists such lusty figures as Omri, Achab, and Jehu. Not to be forgotten is Queen Jezebel. In the middle of the ninth century on one of Ephraim's loveliest green hills was placed the crown

that was Samaria, capital of the north. Reminiscences of
its splendor have been dug up in excavations there, notably
the Samaritan ivories. We have mentioned earlier the
Samaritan ostraca.

Palestine was now a cluster of petty states, Israel, Juda,
Edom, Moab, Aram—either warring with one another or
joining forces to face the threat of Assyria. Egypt, unable
to match Assyrian military power, resorted to inciting in-
trigue and rebellion in the buffer states. The biblical
history of this period receives interesting confirmation in
the records of other countries. The name of King Omri
(c. 876–869 B.C.), founder of Samaria, appears on the
Moabite stone. Jehu (841–814 B.C.), tenth king of Israel,
is named on the black obelisk of Shalmaneser III. Foreign
alliances brought in their wake court marriages, and foreign queens brought alien gods to Israel. When Jezebel
came from Tyre to be wife to Achab, she came with her
gods Baal and Asherah, and their prophets ate at Achab's
table. Israel became infested with idolatrous shrines, at
Dan and Bethel and on every green hill. At the idolatrous
shrines the Israelites lay with the temple prostitutes in the
worship of the goddess of fertility.

The history of the divided kingdom is related in 1 Kings
12–2 Kings 17. This is the period when the writing
prophets emerge in the history of Israel. These prophets
continue in the great prophetic tradition, the difference
being that their prophecies are preserved in writing. The
character of the prophet is seen in Nathan in the days of

King David. The prophet in Israel was an instrument of Yahweh, a charismatic figure as was the king. He was the spokesman for Yahweh, making known his will to the ruler and to the people. At God's direction Nathan reversed David's plan to build a temple (2 Sam. 7). He denounced the king to his face for the crime he committed against Urias and his adultery with Bethsabee, his wife, and David bowed to the expression of the Lord's will (2 Sam. 12).

In the days of King Achab, Elias was the prophet of the Lord and the indomitable champion of his cause against the forces of Baalism. The cycle of Elias (1 Kings 17-2 Kings 1) is a masterpiece of literary art, composed very likely toward the end of the ninth century. The uncompromising faith of Elias is dramatically depicted in his contest with the prophets of Baal at the Wady Kishon. It resounds in his undying words: "If the Lord [Yahweh] be God follow him; but if Baal, then follow him" (1 Kings 18:21). Loyalty to the Lord was the mark of the prophet, as was fidelity to man, especially to the poor and the oppressed. The wrath of the prophet would burn at the social injustice of the king. When Achab and Jezebel were guilty of injustice to Naboth by dispossessing him of his vineyard and slaying him, Elias confronted them with the wrathful word of God, "Thus saith the Lord: Thou hast slain, moreover, also thou hast taken possession. . . . In this place, wherein the dogs have licked the blood of Naboth, they shall lick thy blood also. . . . The dogs shall eat Jezebel in the field of Jezrael" (1 Kings 21:19, 23).

The writing prophets of the period prior to the fall of Samaria in 722 B.C. were Osee and Amos in the kingdom of Israel; Micheas and Isaias in the kingdom of Juda. Amos and Osee were prophets in the day of Israel's greatest prosperity under Jeroboam II (783–743 B.C.). Dan and Bethel were by this time thriving sanctuaries of bull-worship. The poor of the land were heavily burdened by the oppression of the court and the wealthy aristocracy. Against this apostasy and these social ills Amos and Osee raised their agonizing voices.

> They have sold the innocent for silver,
> And the needy in exchange for a pair of sandals;
> They who trample upon the heads of the poor.
> (Amos 2:6 f.)
> A maker of images is Ephraim
> He has set up for himself a fat bull.
> (Osee 4:17)

The prophetic message was that the Lord was not one to countenance idolatry and social injustice. Both are infidelities in his sight. Nor was he one to be put off by rites and sacrifices unattended by moral virtue.

> For I delight in piety, not sacrifice;
> And in knowledge of God, rather than burnt offerings.
> (Osee 6:6)

The prophet saw one law of God's world as inescapable: moral degradation of a nation is the path to its destruction.

> I am your destruction, O Israel
> Who can help you?
> (Osee 13:9)
> Ephraim shall become a ruin
> on the day of judgement.
> (Osee 5:9)
> For they sowed the wind;
> And they shall reap the whirlwind.
> (Osee 8:7)

He proclaimed that there was only one hope of recall from this road to national disaster.

> Return, O Israel, to the Lord [Yahweh] your God.
> (Osee 14:1)

The prophet foresaw that there would be no return and that the doom was inevitable, but did not abandon hope:

> And I will destroy it from off the face of the earth,
> Except that I will not wholly destroy the house of Jacob.
> The oracle of the Lord.
> (Amos 9:8)

For the prophets there always abides the Messianic hope. The people of God will not utterly be destroyed, for the prophets remember the covenant of the Lord. The God of Israel is the God of love:

> When Israel was a child I came to love him,
>> And from Egypt I called him.
>
> . . . . . . . . . . . . . . . . .
>
> But they did not know that I cared for them.
>> With human lines I led them,
>>> With loving cords.
>>>> (Osee 11:3 f.)

The same preoccupation with man's injustice to man is encountered in Micheas, prophet in Juda (cf. 2:1–11). Like Amos and Osee he predicted the doom to come upon Israel and upon Juda as well (1:2–9), but his threats were balanced by promises. In Chapters 4–5 he presents the Messianic concept of the "remnant." This is also a notable aspect of the preaching of Isaias. According to this teaching the recipient of the Messianic hope will not be the nation as such, but a portion of it that will survive the impending disaster to become a spiritual elite. This aspect of Micheas' teaching is a further development of the royal Messianism that we met first in 2 Samuel 7. It is expressed in Micheas 5:2–4, where the prophet links the Messianic hope with Bethlehem (Ephrata), that is, the place of origin of the family of David.

The prophetic activity of Isaias in Juda began before the fall of Samaria and extended to the deliverance of Jerusalem from the armies of Sennacherib in 701 B.C., covering a period of forty years. The prophecies that date from this period are found in Isaias 1–35. Isaias of Jerusa-

lem stands with the author of Job as the greatest of Old
Testament poets. Some of the loveliest literary expressions
of the Bible are found in the book—for example, the Song
of the Vineyard (5:1–7). But Isaias is remembered rightly
as the greatest of the prophets. The same burning fervor
for social justice flames in him as in Amos and Osee.

> Your hands are full of bloodshed—
> wash yourselves clean;
> Put away the evil of your doings
> from before my eyes;
> Cease to do evil,
> learn to do good;
> Seek justice
> restrain the oppressor;
> Uphold the rights of the orphan,
> defend the cause of the widow. (1:15–17)

Isaias foretold the doom of Israel as did his predecessors.

> And the proud crown of the drunkards of Ephraim
> Will be trampled under foot. (28:3)

He warned Juda that a similar fate awaited her for her
wickedness.

> For a sentence of doom, complete and decisive,
> Have I heard from the Lord, the Lord of hosts. (28:22)

But the divine purposes were not to be frustrated by
Israel's infidelities, for a "remnant" would be saved. This
significant aspect of Isaias' message had a living expression

in one of his sons, whom he named Shear-Yasub ("a remnant will return"). From 8:16 it appears that we meet a new development in the history of Old Testament religion. The words "I will bind up my testimony and seal my teaching in the heart of my disciples" are interpreted to mark the beginning of the prophetic party, a spiritual community distinct from the national community, through which the divine designs will one day be accomplished.

The best known of the Isaian texts are probably those of the "book of Emmanuel" (6–9), which belongs to the period of the Syro-Ephraimite league against Juda. The kings of Syria and Israel, allied against Assyria, plotted to overthrow King Achaz and replace him with a king of their own choosing. This was a threat to the dynasty of David, and Isaias viewed the threat in light of Nathan's oracle to David (2 Sam. 7). He saw the Messianic hope of deliverance bound up with the dynasty by virtue of the Davidic covenant. Therefore he declared that the plot of the "two stumps of smoking firebrands" would come to naught. It is in the context of royal Messianism that 7:14, 9:1–6 (the Prince of Peace), and 11:1–15 (the Righteous King) should be read. The reader will then perceive the historical roots of Isaias' Messianism and glimpse the sweeping horizons that touch the figure of Jesus and the Messianic kingdom of Christ which the Evangelists and Christian tradition behold in these texts.

We must not take leave of the great prophet without a

word about his concept of God. We encounter it in the dramatic inaugural vision of Isaias 6. The Seraphim cover their faces with their wings, for they dare not look upon the Lord of glory. They can only repeat, "Holy, holy, holy." To Isaias the Lord is "The Holy One," that is, the One wholly apart, the One who dwells in inaccessible majesty and ineffable mystery, the transcendent One. Yet this is the very One who condescends to be "The Holy One of Israel"; who can speak through his prophet such loving words as the Song of the Vineyard. With what sure touch the Church chose the words of Isaias 6:3 and placed them in the Mass, that never their sound may cease, nor the holiness of God be forgotten.

SEVEN

# THE DECLINE AND FALL OF JUDA

Israel was no more. The lesson of her tragic history loomed large to the Deuteronomist editor. His indictment of the nation resounds in 2 Kings 17. Israel "forsook all the precepts of the Lord their God; and made to themselves two molten calves and groves, and adored all the host of heaven, and they served Baal, and consecrated their sons and daughters through fire. . . . And the Lord was very angry with Israel, and removed them from his sight, and there remained only the tribe of Juda" (17:16–18).

The remaining chapters of 2 Kings (18–25) relate the

history of the kings of Juda to the time of its downfall.
When Samaria fell in 722 B.C. Ezechias was king in Juda.
His capital was threatened by the armies of Sennacherib
in 701 B.C. after he "rebelled against the king of Assyria
and served him not" (2 Kings 18:7). During this crisis
the prophet Isaias appears in the historical record. In
answer to the king's appeal, Isaias foretold, "Thus saith
the Lord . . . 'Behold I will send a spirit upon him [Sen-
nacherib], and he shall hear a message, and shall return
into his own country, and I will make him fall by the
sword in his own country'" (2 Kings 19:6–7). In keeping
with the prediction of Isaias, it came to pass that "an angel
of the Lord" destroyed the besieging Assyrians. "Angel"
in this context is very likely a symbolic expression for
plague. Herodotus relates that the debacle was due to field
mice that devoured the enemy's weapons and spread
bubonic plague. The biblical account of the siege is sup-
plemented by the Assyrian records. On a hexagonal prism
inscribed in cuneiform, Sennacherib boasts, "[Ezechias] I
imprisoned in Jerusalem, his residence, like a bird in its
cage. I surrounded him with earthworks in order to punish
the temerity of any man who dared to come out of the
city gate." There is no mention of the withdrawal.
Oriental kings did not boast of their embarrassments.

In the crisis Ezechias prayed. The beautiful expression
of his faith is recorded in 2 Kings 19. "O Lord God of
Israel, who sitteth upon the Cherubim [a reference to the
invisible presence of Yahweh in the Holy of Holies],

thou alone art the God of all the kings of the earth; thou madest heaven and earth; incline thy ear and hear; open, O Lord, thy eyes, and see and hear all the words of Sennacherib, who has sent to upbraid unto us the living God . . . . Now, therefore, O Lord, our God, save us from his hand that all the kingdoms of the earth may know that thou art the Lord, the only God" (19:15–19). The lofty concept of God is noteworthy. In Isaias 38:9–20 a lovely psalm reminiscent of the thought of Job is attributed to the pious king.

The Deuteronomist could pay no greater tribute to Ezechias than to compare him to his forefather David. His judgment on the good king was, "And he did that which was good before the Lord, according to all that David his father had done . . . . He trusted in the Lord the God of Israel, so that after him there was none like him among all the kings of Juda, nor any of them that were before him" (2 Kings 18:3. 5).

The chronicle speaks briefly of the reigns of the two impious kings that followed Ezechias. Of Manasses (687–642 B.C.) it is said "he did evil in the sight of the Lord," and the same indictment is given Amon (642–640 B.C.). National disaster for Juda would be the outcome of impiety. "Behold I will bring on evils upon Jerusalem and Juda, that whosoever shall hear of them, both his ears shall tingle" (2 Kings 21:12). The payment of tribute to Assyria by Manasses is recorded in the annals of Esarhaddon and Ashurbanipal.

Josias (640–609 B.C.) was the last of the great kings of Juda. His reign was outstanding for the religious reform based on the book of the Law found in the Temple in 621 B.C. On the basis of this book "the king . . . made a covenant with the Lord . . . and the people agreed to the covenant" (2 Kings 23:3). He waged a war of extermination upon the idolatrous cult centers that flourished everywhere, tore down the sanctuaries of the goddess of fertility, of Baal, of the worshipers of the sun and moon and all the hosts of heaven. The reform carried to Bethel and to the high places of Samaria. The king commanded the people to keep the Passover, and we are told that "There was no such Passover kept from the days of the judges . . . nor in all the days of the kings of Israel and of the kings of Juda" (2 Kings 23: 22).

The event that led to the reform of Josias, the finding of the book of the Law, has great significance in Pentateuch criticism. Comparative study of the lines of Josias' reform and the prescriptions in the code of laws that is at the heart of Deuteronomy (12–26) have led to the conclusion that the book actually dates from the reign of King Josias and is one of the four documents or sources that make up the Pentateuch, the D document.

When Josias came to the throne in Jerusalem at the age of eight, Ashurbanipal had occupied the throne in Nineveh for almost thirty years. His reign marked the apogee of Assyrian power and prosperity. Trade, art, and literature flourished. We are not left to imagine what the flowering of this art was like. Assyrian bas-reliefs are mounted on the walls of the British Museum for all to see. Ashurbanipal's library at Nineveh has given up to the excavators twenty thousand cuneiform clay tablets. The gifted Assyrian king died in 626 B.C., and fifteen years later one might look in vain for Assyria on a map of the Near East. Nineveh had fallen in 612 B.C. and with it the empire of Assyria.

The Medes and the Chaldeans took over, and the destiny of Juda was tied up with the latter. Egypt, fearful of the rising power of Babylon, came to the aid of fading Assyria. Josias of Juda led his army to the Megiddo pass to intercept the army of Pharaoh. He died there in battle in 609 B.C. Four years later the Egyptians were defeated by Nabuchodonosor, and in 602 he captured Jerusalem. In 598 B.C. the first exiles went out of Jerusalem and in 586 came Juda's fall. Nabuchodonosor razed the city and leveled the Temple, and the words of Jeremias were fulfilled: "Thus says the Lord: Behold I am giving this city into the hand of the king of Babylon, and he shall burn it with fire" (34:2).

To this period belong the prophecies of Sophonias, Nahum, and Habacuc. The activity of Nahum was prior to the fall of Nineveh. His short book of prophecies against Assyria is marked with intense nationalism. The book of Habacuc was probably composed just before the fall of Jerusalem. The prophecies of Sophonias date from the early years of Josias' reign, prior to the reform of 621 B.C. He vividly depicts the religious decadence of Juda and Jerusalem.

> And from this place I shall cut off the Baal to the
>     last remnant;
> The name of the priestlings along with the priests,
> And those who prostrate themselves upon the roofs
> To the host of heaven,
> And those who prostrate themselves before the Lord
> And swear by Milcom. (1:4–5)

He foretells the downfall of mighty Assyria.

> And he [Yahweh] will stretch out his hand against
>     the north and destroy Assyria;
> And he will make Nineveh a desolation,
>     a drought like the desert. (2:13)

The idea of the "Day of the Lord" that appears in Amos 5:18 and Isaias 2:7 ff. is given a cosmic dimension by Sophonias.

> On the day of the wrath of the Lord
>     and in the fire of his zeal,
> All the earth shall be consumed;
> For a complete destruction, indeed a frightful
>     one will he make
> Of all the inhabitants of the earth. (1:18)[1]

---

1 The hymn *Dies Irae* was inspired by Sophonias 1:15. See the verse in the Latin Vulgate.

An even more significant Messianic development is due to Sophonias. After speaking of the wrath of the day of the Lord the prophet appeals in 2:3 to the poor (*anawim*) of the earth to "seek the Lord," to seek "righteousness" and "humility." Thus they may be "hidden" or saved on the day of the Lord. In 3:12 f. "the remnant of Israel" is identified with "a people humble and poor." Sophonias thus places the *anawim* in an eschatological framework, the day of Lord's visitation.

The career of Jeremias the prophet was enacted in that dramatic time in the history of the Near East and of Juda. His ministry began a few years before the reform of Josias in 621. With the fall of Nineveh the Assyrian empire expired in 612. In 609 King Josias, from whom so many had hoped for so much, died in battle at Megiddo. In 598 the Chaldeans besieged Jerusalem and deported part of its population. In 586 Jerusalem and the Temple of Solomon were brought low and the second deportation followed. These were the high and tragic events in which the prophet's lot was cast; this was the din amidst which his voice was heard. He remained on in Jerusalem after the destruction, but later he was forced to go to Egypt and probably died in that alien land.

The book of Jeremias is stamped with the mark of those troubled times. The literary character of the book is complex. Its two principal witnesses, the Hebrew text and the Septuagint Greek manifest significant differences. The latter is notably shorter and has a different order in some

places. In the judgment of critics the book has undergone
a series of editings. The final editing to which it owes its
present form was probably done at the time of the Exile.

Jeremias stands in the great tradition of these prophets
who went before him. Like Osee he is a man of sensitivity;
like Amos he is indignant at social injustice; like Isaias he
is a poet of eloquence as well as a prophet whose faith and
loyalty light up the spiritual darkness. The burden of his
message was the destruction inevitably to come if priests,
princes, and people did not repent their evil ways. We read
in 7:1–15 the account of Jeremias' prediction of the destruction of the Temple. The people trusted in the power
of the Temple to save them, saying, "The temple of the
Lord, the temple of the Lord, the temple of the Lord is
this!" (7:4). To the prophet, hope in the temple of the
Lord was vain without moral righteousness. "Amend your
ways and your doings" was the demand of the Lord (7:3).
This was the oracle of Yahweh: "I will do to this house
which bears my name . . . as I did to Shiloh" (7:14).
Shiloh, the sanctuary of early Israel, was a desolation. To
the people, the princes, and the priests the prediction of
Jeremias was a scandal. For them the temple of the invisible presence of Yahweh was inviolable. Had it not been
a talisman against the hosts of Sennacherib in 701? To
Jeremias this was a fallacious confidence; without righteousness the Temple together with the people would go
down to destruction.

Such preaching could not be popular. In Chapter 26

we find another account of the prediction and its con-
sequences—a biographical sketch, probably from the hand
of Baruch. There the reaction to the message is described:
"The priests and the prophets laid hold of him saying, 'You
shall die! How dare you prophesy in the name of the Lord,
saying, "This house shall become like Shiloh, and this city
shall become an uninhabited waste"?'" (26:8–9). These
passages serve to illustrate the character of the preaching
of Jeremias and the opposition of the people to his message. The situation may serve as a key to understanding the
very significant passages of the book, autobiographical
in character, which reveal the personal feelings of the
prophet, passages that have great importance in the history of Old Testament religion. Comparison of the two
passages may also serve to illustrate the editing process
mentioned above.

Here is an example of the autobiographical style of the
Bible of which Jeremias is considered the creator.

> I have become a laughing-stock all day long,
> Everyone mocks at me.
> As often as I speak, I must cry out,
> I must call, Violence and spoil!
> For the word of the Lord has become to me
> A reproach and derision all day long.
>
> If I say, I will not think of it,
> Nor speak any more in his name,
> It is in my heart like a burning fire,

Shut up in my bones;
I am worn out with holding it in,
I cannot endure it. (20:7–9)

The style is introspective, revealing the prophet's inner feelings of sensitivity. The suffering of the prophet led him to open his heart to God, to come to that conversation with God which is the essence of individual spirituality. This direction in Jeremias looks to the spirit of the New Testament.

The peak of the prophetic revelation of Jeremias is to see interior religion as a condition of Messianic times. "Behold, days are coming, is the oracle of the Lord, when I will make a new covenant with the house of Israel and with the house of Juda, not like the covenant I made with their fathers" (31:31 f.). It will be a new covenant because it will be interior. ("I will put my law within them and will write it on their hearts." 31:33) God will give them a "new heart" (32:39) "to know" the Lord (24:7).

It is the personal religion of Jeremias that brings him close to us, inheritors of the new covenant that he announced. Scholars have noted the influence of Jeremias on Ezechiel, on the second part of Isaias, and on the Psalms. His prestige increased after his death, and he became father of that Jewish piety that finds such authentic religious expression in "the psalms of the poor."

The prophetic ministry of Ezechiel extended from 593 to 571 B.C. He was taken from Jerusalem in the deportation of 598 B.C. It seems that the book of Ezechiel has undergone a series of editings, as is so often the case in the prophetic books. The unity and authenticity of the book are generally accepted by Old Testament critics, allowing for the later editing that did not alter the earlier literary material.

Ezechiel was priest, prophet, and visionary. The major concern of the priest was for the Temple. He was shocked by the idolatrous cults that defiled it (8). He beheld the glory of God depart from it (10) and foresaw it returning to the future Temple (43). He was solicitous for the Law and the Sabbath. His language is similar to that of the Law of Holiness, Leviticus 17–26, heart of the Priestly Code of the Pentateuch. The prophet synthesizes in his complex personality two forces frequently in tension, the priest and the prophet.

There is a marked affinity between Ezechiel and Jeremias. Both share the sense of despair for Juda, the hope for the exiles, the confidence in a future return. Both speak of a second David who will come to rule the restored community (Ezech. 34:23 f.; Jer. 23:5 f.). Both stress individual responsibility (Ezech. 18). We have underscored above the emphasis in Jeremias on the "new heart." This idea is at the center of the message of Ezechiel. "I will give you a new heart, and will put within you a new spirit; I will remove the heart of stone out of your flesh and will give you a heart of flesh; and I will put my spirit within you, and make you follow my statutes and be care-

ful to observe my ordinances. You shall live in the land
which I gave to your fathers; and you shall be my people
and I will be your God" (36:26–28).

According to Ezechiel the "remnant" that will return
is the qualitative Israel, the spiritual core of the nation
purified by the experience of the Exile, renewed in spirit
by the "new heart" and dedicated to moral living. The
prophet is acutely aware of the "holiness" of God, and is
awe-struck by it. His concept of holiness is similar to what
we term divine transcendence. An important part of
Ezechiel's thesis is that Yahweh will vindicate his "holiness" before all the world by restoration of Israel. Never is
the prophet unaware of the nothingness of man in comparison with God. Eighty-seven times in the book we encounter the expression "son of man," meaning man as
mortal.

Ezechiel was a visionary. His imagery at times will appear to the reader as fantastic and unintelligible. It is possible that it was influenced by the art of Babylonia, with
the winged creatures that adorned its gates and palaces
(cf. 1:1–3:15). He was an ecstatic visionary experiencing
at times mystical rapture akin to the experiences St. Paul
describes in his letters. Another characteristic feature of
his literary art is the allegorical tableau. The best known
of these is the allegory of the dry bones in 37:1–14, which
has been dramatized in a Negro spiritual.

Ezechiel's influence in the development of Judaism is
most significant. He has in fact been called "the father of

Judaism." First of all there is his influence on the priestly circle, confirmed by the relationship of his book to the Priestly Code. The emphasis that was found in Judaism on the Temple and the Torah can be traced to Ezechiel. The apocalyptic writers of the last two pre-Christian centuries were influenced in their imagery by the visionary style of Ezechiel. The Jewish sages, like the author of Job, took up the problem of retribution raised by the prophet. Jesus spoke in the accents of Ezechiel when he described himself as the shepherd seeking the lost sheep (Ezech. 34).

# EIGHT

## THE RESTORATION

How lonely the city sits,
　　once so crowded with people!
· · · · · · · · · · · · · · · · · ·
The roads to Sion mourn,
　　without pilgrims to the feast.
　　　　　　　　Lamentations 1:1.4

These words evoke the image of Jerusalem after 586 B.C.,
broken and desolate. The words are taken from the book
of Lamentations, mournful dirges uttered over the ruins
of the city. It is quite likely that they were composed after

the destruction and served for a liturgy that was enacted in the charred and shattered remains of the Temple of Solomon. This would remind one of the mournful prayers of pious Jews at the Wailing Wall in Jerusalem. The Wailing Wall is the few tiers of stones that are left of the Herod Temple destroyed by the Romans in A.D. 70.

It is almost impossible to imagine what the disaster of 586 meant to the faithful Jew. He believed that God's designs in history were bound up with his nation, with the dynasty of David, with Sion and its Temple. What of God's designs and Israel's destiny now? Fuller realization would come with the prophetic instruction of Jeremias and Ezechiel. The prophets guided Juda to the understanding of its destiny. Under the harsh blows of historical events and by the chastisement of the Exile they were transformed. They would not return to the habits of their idolatrous past. They would turn away from dreams of empire to visions of religious values. This would not happen all at once and to everyone. Something of the nation was left in Juda, but the true Israel was in Babylonia, and in its midst was the core of religious idealism that would inspire the return when the time came.

> Comfort, O comfort my people,
>     says your God;
> Speak to the heart of Jerusalem,
>     and call to her.

That her time of service is ended,
    that her guilt is paid in full,
That she has received from the Lord's hand
    double for all her sins. (Is. 40:1 f.)

So begins the second part of the book of Isaias, described as the book of the consolation of Israel. This part of the book, 40–55, brings up one of the most celebrated questions of Old Testament criticism, namely, the authorship and date of this section. It is not to our purpose to describe this critical question at length, for the average reader of the Scriptures is only moderately interested in the details of higher criticism. The interpretation is, however, conditioned by critical conclusions, and therefore a brief note on the matter would seem to be in order.

This is the critical problem that this section poses: The prophet seems to speak to an audience living amid the historical events of the sixth century; Jerusalem has fallen, the people are in Exile, Cyrus the Persian is already on stage, and the speaker's point of interest is the end of the Exile. No critic will deny that the author addresses the Jews of the sixth century. The alternatives are that he lived in that century either *prophetically* or *actually*. If one holds that the author is Isaias of the eighth century, he must conclude that the prophet projected himself ideally into the sixth century. It must be conceded that this view makes great demands of its adherents, given the literary character of this section. The opposite view, without denying the prophet's capacity to predict, asserts that prophetic prediction is always related to the prophet's message to his contemporaries and insists that the message of 40–55 is addressed to the Jews in exile as contemporaries, not as a generation to come.

A distinction must be made between Catholic and non-Catholic critics. Centuries of tradition attributing the entire book to the eighth-century Isaias inclined Catholic critics to be conservative in adopting the view of an anonymous author of this section—a Second Isaias. In fact, the Biblical Commission discouraged the direction by its decree of June 28, 1908. It was not the intention of the Commission to shut the door on subsequent critical investigation by Catholic scholars. The great growth of knowledge during the past fifty years has altered the situation since the Commission published its decree. An increasing number of Catholic critics endorse the view of a Second Isaias as highly probable. This is the position taken in the Bible of Jerusalem.

The historical event that led to the end of the Exile was Persia's rise to power with the victories of Cyrus II (557–529 B.C.). Cyrus invaded Babylonia in 539 B.C. and subjugated it with the fall of Babylon. This marked the end of the Chaldean or Neo-Babylonian empire. The new empire of the Aryans would one day create the splendor of Persepolis and produce the great Darius I, who left an inscription high in the rocks of Behistun. The important thing to note here, however, was the policy of Cyrus as opposed to that of the Assyrians and Babylonians before him. He pursued a policy of conciliation by honoring the gods of conquered nations and respecting their customs. In 538 B.C. he authorized the Jewish exiles to return to their homeland and rebuild their temple to their God.

To the author of Deutero-Isaias, Cyrus is the instrument of the Lord. He is called his "anointed" (Messias) in 45:1. The fall of Babylon is depicted in Chapter 47. ("Come down, and sit in the dust, O virgin daughter of Babylon, Sit throneless on the earth, O daughter of the Chaldeans!") Then the new Exodus will take place, greater even than the first, as Juda returns across the Syrian desert to Jerusalem (41:17–19; 43:19–20). The Israel that returned was a people spiritually transformed, the qualitative Israel that the Lord calls his servant. When this Israel occupies Jerusalem, God will reign there; the heathen nations will be astonished at his power and glory and will come to join Israel (55:4–5).

In addition to the theme of a glorious restoration there is a second theme in this section of very great interest. In four passages the work of the kingdom of God is related to the suffering of what seems to be a mysterious individual. He is called simply "Servant." The passages in question are 42:1–4; 49:1–6; 50:4–9; 52:13–53:12. Two questions are discussed in regard to these passages. The first is their literary relationship to the section (40–55) in which they are found. The greater number of critics consider them four separate songs. There is still some discussion as to the precise extent of each song. A question of greater importance to the Bible reader is their interpretation, which may recall to him the dilemma of the Ethiopian eunuch of Candace to whom Philip was so obliging (Acts 8:26–39). The undeviating position of Jewish scholarship is that the Servant here as elsewhere is Israel. Christian scholarship favors the individual interpretation, this particularly in the last song (52:13–53:12), which is a startling anticipation of the suffering of Jesus, a passage most prominent in the liturgy of Holy Week.

The disaster of 586 B.C. marks a turning point in the history of Israel. Out of the experience of the catastrophe and the Exile, the Jewish community was to be born, a community in which religious values were placed above national interests. The Exile is of great significance in the literary development of the Old Testament and in the doctrinal development as well. The Chaldeans had not deported every citizen of Juda to a man. A shabby remnant was left. The social and religious elite went into exile. There were opportunities in Babylonia for those who sought them. For some, prosperity in Babylonia was destiny enough. But there was a core of religious idealists, the little remnant. They would serve to carry out the divine design for mankind. Under the guidance of Ezechiel and Isaias (40–55) they would be formed into a community in the Exile that kept its identity by virtue of its religious ideals. The God in whom they believed was able to raise them up out of the graves of the Exile and restore them to life and to their country (Ezech. 37:1-14). They learned that their faith could endure far from the Promised Land, without the Temple of Solomon. Faith in God and fidelity to the Law of Moses was enough to sustain them. In those decades, therefore, the hope of Israel was in Babylonia; and the hope of mankind.

The remnant returned home. The first return was in 538 B.C. under the leadership of Zorobabel, the second and third in 445 and 398 under Esdras and Nehemias. This history is related in the books of Esdras and Nehemias (1-2 Esdras). They do not pretend to give a complete history of the period, but the religious significance of history. The basic work, originally one undivided book, was written shortly after the return. Critics judge that the present form dates from about 300 B.C., when it was edited as part of a larger work that included Chronicles (Paralipomenon).

There are three principal themes in Esdras-Nehemias: the reconstruction of the Temple (Esd. 1-6, except 4:6-23); the restoration of the city of Jerusalem (Esd. 4:6-23; Neh. 1-13); the establishment of Judaism on its juridical foundations (Esd. 7-10). The first attempts at rebuilding the Temple were prevented by the opposition of the Samaritans. It was completed during the reign of Darius (521-486 B.C.), and the Passover was celebrated. Due to the persistent efforts of Nehemias and with the backing of the Persian court, the walls of Jerusalem were at length rebuilt (Neh. 2:12–4:23). The more difficult task of re-establishing the reign of the Torah was accomplished by Esdras and Nehemias, and the people bound themselves to observe it by a renewed covenant (Neh. 8:1–10:39).

One aspect of this juridical reform has particular significance—the suppression of mixed marriage, that is, marriages of Jews with foreigners. An outstanding characteristic of the restored community was separatism, of which this is an example. Here then are the essential elements of the post-exilic religion called Judaism: Jerusalem rebuilt as the center of a small theocratic community, bound by covenant to observe the Torah, enacting its ritual in the Second Temple.

Two of the Minor Prophets belong in this historical context, Aggeus (Haggai) and Zacharias. They were both active in the community about 520 B.C. Aggeus' interest is in the Temple. After the first bursts of enthusiasm, apathy had set in. The prophets encouraged the people to finish the task. The structure was completed in 520 B.C. Aggeus said of it, "The future splendor of this house shall be greater than the past" (2:9). The first section of Zacharias (1–8) fits this historical context, but the last section (9–14) seems to belong to a later period, at least in its final editing. This section is notable for its Messianic teaching, such well-known and well-loved texts as these.

Exult greatly, O daughter of Sion;
Shout with joy, O daughter of Jerusalem.
Lo, your king comes to you;

. . . . . . . . . . . . . . . .

Humble and riding upon an ass. (9:9)

"And I will pour out upon the house of David and upon
the inhabitants of Jerusalem a spirit of favor and of prayer;
and they look upon him whom they have pierced, and
they shall mourn for him like the mourning for an only
child" (12:10).

It is little wonder that these texts should be quoted in
the New Testament (Matt. 21:4 f.; 27:9; 26:31). Certain themes emphasized by Aggeus and Zacharias reveal
the influence of Ezechiel's thought—the emphasis on the
Temple, on ritualistic purity, on angels. The last section
of Isaias (56–66) should be read in this historical context.
Putting aside critical questions concerning the date and
authorship of the section, it is addressed to the Jews returned from the Exile.

Other minor prophets belong to this period, the fifth
and fourth pre-Christian centuries. They are Malachias,
Joel, Abdias, and Jonas. Abdias (Obadiah), the shortest
of the prophetic books, is strongly nationalistic in tone.
The preoccupation of Malachias is the sins of priests and
people in the matter of cult, the scandal of mixed marriages and divorce. In contrast to the imperfect sacrifices
the prophet speaks of the perfect sacrifice of the Messianic

age in 1:11—a text which the Church sees fulfilled in the Sacrifice of the Mass.

> For from the rising of the sun, even to its setting
> My name is great among the nations;
> And in every place an incense offering
>       is presented to my name,
> And a pure offering,
> For my name is great among the nations.

The book of Joel is characterized by the same emphasis noted in Ezechiel and the post-exilic prophets. A new Messianic note is sounded in Joel 2:28.

> It shall come to pass afterward
> That I will pour out my spirit upon all flesh;
> Your sons and your daughters shall prophesy.
> Your old men shall dream dreams,
> And your young men shall see visions.

Joel had been called the prophet of Pentecost. St. Peter quoted these words in his preaching on the first Pentecost.

The book of Jonas is in another category altogether. It is not a collection of a prophet's preachings and oracles, but a story. Many features of the book lead one to believe that it is a fictional story created to teach a moral lesson, and that it was far from the inspired author's intention that it be taken literally. The sudden conversion of the king of Nineveh and all his people to the God of Israel is a real strain on credibility, not to speak of Jonas in the belly of the big fish. It would seem that the book should rather be considered as a piece of satire, cleverly teaching the separatist Jews a lesson in universalism: All the world is sympathetic except Juda. They need contrite hearts like the Ninevites in the story! The New Testament references to the book would not seem to demand that it be considered historical, any more than an allusion to Hamlet can be considered an argument for his existence.

The Persian empire survived for two centuries. They were centuries of respite for the little community of Juda, centuries in which the forces that made up Judaism solidified. Jerusalem was the religious capital not only for the Jews of Palestine, but for Jews throughout the world. The Temple was its heart and center of its worship. The Torah was the law supreme, guide of social, political, economic, and personal life. The mark of Jewish piety was holiness, freedom from defilement, because God was holy. The idea of God as holy deepened so as to make God seem too transcendent. With the conquest of Hellenism, this way of life was to confront a new and dynamic threat in the alluring culture of Greece.

Alexander the Great died at thirty-three in 323 B.C. By that time he had conquered the civilized world. His dreams of empire were not visions of conquered peoples cowering under bristling arms, but of happy people enamored of the culture of Greece. Hard upon the heels of the conquering warriors came the colonists. Cities were set up according to the Greek ideal. The physical character of

these cities can be discerned in ruins like Jerash in Jordan.
The Decapolis, meaning a league of ten free cities, is an
expression found in the New Testament. Soon the civilized world woke up to find itself Greek. The language
and the cultural way of Greece had invaded with Alexander and his successors.

After the death of Alexander the empire was divided
among his generals. Syria fell to Seleucus, who gave his
name to the Seleucid dynasty. Ptolemy, ruler in Egypt,
was father to the line of Ptolemies. To these Juda was
first subject, and the tranquility of her ways was unmolested. This situation was not without hazards, for it
allowed for peaceful yet insidious penetration of Hellenism, which might in time undermine Judaism. The situation changed with the advent to power of the Seleucid
Antiochus iv in 175 B.C. By now Juda was subject to the
Seleucids; the program of Antiochus was to force Hellenism upon the Jews, and to this end he set in motion an
all-out persecution. It was counteracted by Jewish resistance that added glorious pages to Jewish history. They
are summed up in the heroic name, the Machabees. Their
story is told in the two books of Machabees.

First Machabees was written in Hebrew, 2 Machabees
in Greek. They differ in their literary character. The former belongs to the category of religious history. At the
beginning of 1 Machabees the confrontation of Hellenism and Judaism is dramatically presented. Hellenism is
personified in Alexander, Judaism in Mathathias, who gives

the signal for revolt. The book relates the heroic exploits of Judas, Jonathan, and Simon Maccabaeus. The name Maccabaeus, first given to Judas, probably means "The Hammer," like the "Martel" attached to Charles, king of the Franks. The motivation of the Jewish warriors was zeal for the Law, the holy Torah. In their hearts religion and nationalism, piety and patriotism, were one. The book embodies the significant themes of Judaism: the divine transcendence, the inviolability of Sion and the Temple.

Second Machabees is professedly a résumé of the five books of Jason of Cyrene, who is not otherwise known. It is not a continuation of 1 Machabees, but runs parallel to it in part, covering about fifteen years of the period, from 175 to 160 B.C. The significance of this book lies in its religious teaching: the resurrection of the dead (7:9. 11. 14. 36, etc.); sanctions after death (6:26; 7:36; 12:45); prayer for the departed (12:43. 44. 46); intercession of the saints (15:12–16). The ideas are important in the development of Old Testament religion and as a preparation for the revelation of Jesus. It is therefore regrettable that this and 1 Machabees are not found in the Protestant Bibles. They are considered extra-canonical and listed among the Apocrypha. In Catholic theology they are canonical, called deuterocanonical as explained earlier.

The book of Daniel according to recent Old Testament criticism should be placed in the context of the persecution of Antiochus, designed to support the faith of the Jews oppressed by the tyrant. The Septuagint, the Vulgate, and modern versions include the book among the four major prophets. The Hebrew Bible does not place it among the prophets but in the third and last section, called the Ketubim, "the writings," in the sense of "the rest of the sacred writings." This point is not without significance in considering the date of the book. It is unusual in being written in two languages, Hebrew and Aramaic. The first part of the book (1–6) differs in character from the second part (7–12). There are three sections in Catholic Bibles that are not found in the Hebrew or Protestant Bibles, the canticles of Azarias and of the three youths in the fiery furnace (3:24–90), the story of Susanna (13), and Bel and the Dragon (14). These are preserved only in Greek and Syrian translations of a highly probable Aramaic original. Despite these literary complexities critics support the unity of the book, apart from the additions.

Before the advent of modern biblical criticism it was traditionally held that the book was the work of Daniel of the sixth century. This position has long since been abandoned by independent critics, and more recently by a growing number of Catholic critics. The fundamental reason for this position is that the book for the most part seems to be a veiled history of events that have happened rather than a prediction of things to come. Chapter 11 provides a key to the problem of date. It depicts in great detail the conflicts between the Seleucids and the Ptolemies, and the advent of Antiochus. This is related in prophetic style, but is quite obviously a record of *faits accomplis.*

In order to elucidate this statement a word about apocalyptic literature is here in order. Jewish apocalyptic is a literary genre that had its florescence in the two centuries before Christ and somewhat after. It is characteristic of this genre that it professes to be a revelation long hidden and now revealed; this is the reason for the name, which comes from the Greek word *apokalupsis,* which means unveiling. The revelation is generally attributed to some notable figure of antiquity—for example, Henoch; it is consequently pseudonymous. It depicts past or present events in esoteric imagery, in a style often fantastic and bizarre. Its chief concern is with future events, particularly the end time.

There is no question but that the second part of Daniel belongs in this genre. This is in no way meant to demean the book, but only accurately to determine its literary genre with a view to proper interpretation. The second section includes the vision of the four beasts (7:1–28), the vision of the ram and the he-goat (8:1–27), the prophecy of the seventy weeks (9:1–27), the great vision of the time of God's wrath and the end time (10–12). This section differs from the first part, which tells about Daniel in the third person in narrative style. The question of the literary genre of this part also merits careful attention. In 5:1 f. Baltassar is said to be a king and son of Nabuchodonosor. Historians say that Baltassar was son of Nabonidus and that he was

never king. Without reviewing the total situation, suffice it
to say that critics conclude that this part of Daniel is not
historical. They judge it to be a *midrash,* that is, a fictional
retelling of the story of Daniel, an elaboration of an historical core. This section is considered didactic in purpose
rather than strictly historical, designed to inspire the
persecuted Jews by the heroic example of the persecuted
Daniel. In light of such considerations critics put the date
of the book between 167 and 164 B.C.

The lasting significance of the book of Daniel lies in its
presentation of a philosophy of history assuring us of the
final triumph of God in his Messias. The struggle described
is the conflict between the heathen empire and the chosen
people. The book has relevance for all ages; particularly
our own, since the onslaughts against the City of God
never cease. One should sedulously avoid twisting the
imagery of Daniel to fit situations never intended by the
author. All too many, even now, engage in this ill-advised
and unscientific endeavor. The beasts and the symbols of
Daniel represent the Chaldeans, the Persians, the Greeks,
and his center of interest is that paragon of persecutors,
Antiochus IV Epiphanes. To interpret these figures in
terms of medieval or contemporary history is to make a
plaything of the Word of God and to employ the venera-
ble authority of the Scripture in the cause of whims and
fancies.

The author of Daniel is the first to view world history
as a preparation for the kingdom of God and to bring

God's designs for men to the very threshold of eternity. The Messias of Daniel is not only the son of David; he is the transcendent Messias (7:13). When Jesus was on trial for his life this was the text he quoted (Matt. 26:64), and the title he preferred for himself during his life was Daniel's "Son of Man."

# NINE

# THE WISDOM OF THE OLD TESTAMENT

In our English Bibles after the historical books of the Old Testament we find the group called didactic. The word is of Greek origin and means teaching or instruction. The inference is that the books contain moral and spiritual instruction. The books are Job, Psalms, Proverbs, Ecclesiastes, Canticle (Song of Solomon), Wisdom, and Sirach (Ecclesiasticus). This is the Catholic listing. The last two are not found in the Jewish or Protestant Bibles. The reasons for this difference were indicated above when we discussed the Palestinian and Alexandrian canons.

Most of these books are better classified in the genre called Wisdom literature (the Canticle would not properly belong to this genre, nor would all of the Psalms, and Job only with some qualification). The pursuit of wisdom was characteristic of the civilizations of the ancient Near East. Our knowledge of the wisdom literature of Mesopotamia, Egypt, and Canaan has increased in recent decades and the Old Testament wisdom has been studied in this historical context. A well-known example of Egyptian wisdom literature is the hieratic text "The Teaching of Amenemope." Scholars have discovered interesting resemblances between this text and the book of Proverbs (see 22:17–23:24). It is difficult to determine with certitude the precise relationship of the two, nor is that necessary here, but the fact is clear that wisdom literature was an international institution in antiquity, and Israel was part of it and influenced by it.

The pursuit of wisdom is a special mark of post-exilic Judaism. The sage takes his place beside the priest and the prophet; with the cessation of prophecy in Juda, the wise man in great measure falls heir to role of the prophet in the religious life of the nation. The reader will be struck by the fact that much of the wisdom writing of the Old Testament is plain common sense dressed up in literary garb. This is true in great part. It has been described aptly as "the wisdom of many and the wit of one." The wisdom of the Old Testament, like the wisdom of the ancient East, is a humanism, but unlike that of the pagan civilizations it breathes the atmosphere of faith in Yahweh.

Israel looked back to Solomon as the father of its wisdom. They said of him, "King Solomon exceeded all the kings of the earth in riches and *wisdom*. All the earth desired to see Solomon's face, to hear his *wisdom* which God had given in his heart" (1 Kings 10:23 f.). It was said that the wise king "spoke three thousand proverbs" (1 Kings 4:32). Some of these are undoubtedly preserved in the book of Proverbs. The proverb is the chief feature of the wisdom literature—the brief sententious expression of the wisdom of many. Here are a few examples from the Book of Proverbs:

> Like golden apples in silver settings
> are words spoken at the proper time. (25:11)

> He who trusts himself is a fool,
> but he who walks in wisdom is safe. (28:26)

A consideration of the individual books of this class will reveal the line of development of Old Testament wisdom and will contribute to the reader's understanding.

The Book of Proverbs holds the highest and the oldest place. It is composite in character and takes its name from its oldest and longest portions, called "The Proverbs of Solomon" (10:1–22:16 and 25:1–29:27). It has been suggested that these go back to the king and were published as a collection about 800 B.C. The book in its final form dates probably from the fifth century. The fact that "wisdom" was a common store of antiquity from which Israel felt free to borrow is seen from 22:19 ("I make known to you the words of Amen-em-Ope."), from 30:1 ("the words of Agur, son of Yakeh the Massaite") and 31:1 ("the words of Lamuel, king of Massa"). Like the wisdom of the nations, Israel's wisdom was founded on experience, but for Israel it was an experience infused with faith in the Lord. At heart they were always disciples of Moses. The ideal the book proposes is a religious humanism in personal, family, and social life, whose reward is success and happiness in this life. That this wisdom is more than pragmatism is seen from the keynote of the book: "The beginning of wisdom is the fear of the Lord" (9:10, etc.).

Wisdom is that quality in man that directs his conduct to its true purpose. Intellectual in origin, it is practical in application, guided by the reverential fear of God. Its source is God. "The Lord gives wisdom" (2:6). God is the everlasting sage. The consideration of God's wisdom calls forth some of the book's noblest expressions. The wisdom that is in God is portrayed as a person and speaks:

The Lord begot me, the firstborn of his ways,
　　the forerunner of his prodigies of long ago;
From of old I was poured forth,
　　at the first, before the earth.
When there were no depths I was brought forth,
　　when there were no fountains or springs of water;

Before the mountains were settled into place,
    before the hills, I was brought forth;
While as yet the earth and the fields were not made,
    nor the first clods of the world.

When he established the heavens I was there,
    when he marked out the vault over the face of the deep;
When he made firm the skies above,
    when he fixed fast the foundations of the earth;
When he set for the sea its limit,
    so that the waters should not transgress his command;
Then was I beside him as his craftsman,
    and I was his delight day by day,
Playing before him all the while,
    playing on the surface of his earth. (8:22–31)

This is an eloquent literary personification of God's wisdom. Is it more than that? Some have felt that there is in these lines a suggestion of the New Testament revelation of the Incarnation, the Word of God described in the prologue of John. We are disinclined to go that far, but reading these lines in light of the New Testament revelation does give them a fuller meaning and the reader a deeper sense of mystery. The Church uses this and other wisdom texts in the Mass and Office of Our Lady. Such liturgical use is obviously not intended to offer a literal interpretation of the texts. It is customary for the liturgy to use biblical texts in an accommodated sense—that is, applying to one what was said of another by reason of the aptness of the expression. It may only be a line of the excerpt that has a special aptness. This can be seen in Sirach 24:12, "He that made me, rested in my tabernacle."[1] The words apply with such aptness to Mary bearing Jesus.

The book of Job is an argument. It is a controversial dialogue framed in great poetry, a contentious drama. The point at issue is the problem that has tantalized wise men of all ages: Why do the innocent suffer? The problem taunted the mind of an ancient poet of Akkad about 2000 B.C. About the time that Job was published, the Greeks were posing the same problem in such tragic figures as Oedipus Rex.

The wisdom that was founded on experience had to be tested by experience; not only the experience of surface observation, but also the inner experience of reflection and conscience. This is what the book of Job brings up for hearing. Job was not a Hebrew; probably an Idumacan. The figure may be a hero of Semitic antiquity. The question of his historicity is not of first importance. In the Hebrew canon the book is placed among the didactic, not the historical, books, and the Talmud considers it fictional. The work is of a complex literary character, but its final editing was probably done about 450 B.C.

Only in light of the Hebrew mentality of the time can

[1] This translation is according to the Douay, which is based on the Latin Vulgate, the text of the liturgy. The correct translation is: "He who formed me [Wisdom] chose the spot for my tent," that is, in the Temple of Jerusalem. Cf. 24:8 Confraternity Edition.

the book of Job be understood. Two aspects of that mentality are relevant, the notion of retribution and the concept of the after-life. The accepted principle of Hebrew wisdom in the time of Job was that God rewards the just and punishes the wicked in this life. That is the wisdom found in Proverbs. The common conception of the after-life was based upon the notion of Sheol. Sheol was the underworld where the departed survived in a very undesirable state of existence. It was believed to be a place of darkness and oblivion, and to go there was not in men's desires. Without distinction the just and the unjust were assembled to endure a shadowy sort of existence. All shared a common lot; the prince was like the pauper, the master like the slave. The dead were cut off from all knowledge of earthly things, and King Ezechias could say to the Lord, "Sheol cannot thank thee, death cannot praise thee" (Is. 38:18).

The idea of retribution in the next life was not part of Job's religious faith. The traditional answer to suffering was that it was a retribution for sin. The protestation of Job's conscience surges from the inner experience of his own innocence. The conflict of the poem is born of Job's inner conviction of his innocence and the accepted wisdom expressed by his comforters, that he is punished because of sin. Job contends that such wisdom does not stand the test of experience, which shows that often the innocent suffer and the wicked prosper. He concludes that the answer eludes man's effort to discern and is with God.

The greatness of Job is in his faith in God, despite the cloud of unknowing.

Proverbs is marked by a serene and optimistic wisdom. Job is branded by protest and conflict, and Ecclesiastes is tainted with melancholy. Ecclesiastes means preacher, or master of wisdom. The book belongs to the Hellenistic period, from the third century most likely, but it does not reflect Hellenistic influence. The preacher is a Jew of Palestine. We may describe him as a healthy Job. He does not have the personal problem of suffering, but he has the experience of the vanity of earthly existence, which is the theme of the book. He has found riches, love, knowledge, and even life wanting. His experience contradicts the traditional wisdom and finds earthly retribution insufficient. The emphasis in the Preacher as in Job is the insufficiency of the present answers. Both push the human spirit to look for fuller wisdom by honestly stating the human problem. The answer to the problems of both is in retribution beyond the grave.

The uncertainties of Job and Ecclesiastes are shared by Jesus Sirach, the author of Ecclesiasticus. The name Ecclesiasticus indicates the fact that the book was officially read in the Church (ecclesiastical). It was written in Hebrew during the Greek period, toward 190 B.C. and is not included in the Hebrew canon, although it is frequently quoted in rabbinical writings and represents the current of Jewish wisdom associated with "the pious" (*Hasidim*) of Palestine, who opposed the forces of heathen Hellenism to the death. It is frequently quoted in the New Testament and in the liturgy. Sirach associates wisdom with the Torah (the Law of Moses), and favors the priesthood and worship. Another distinguishing mark is that he ponders the history of Israel to confirm the faith of his people in the God of the covenant (44–49).

The culmination of the development of wisdom did not come from Jerusalem but from Alexandria, a city dominated by the ideal Alexander furthered: Greek culture. It was also the great center of the Jewish Dispersion. There about the middle of the first century B.C. an unknown Jew wrote in Greek the book of Wisdom. His thought is linked to the wisdom tradition of his forefathers, but it goes beyond them in admitting the value of Greek philosophy, especially the philosophy of Plato. The book was not received into the Palestinian canon, but was part of the Septuagint and is highly favored by the New Testament writers, the Fathers, and the liturgy.

Its significance lies in its solution to the problem of retribution that preoccupied the sages for centuries. It affirmed that God made man for immortality (2:23) and that the recompense for wisdom is blessed immortality with God (5:15 f.). This life is a preparation for the next life, where the just are rewarded and the wicked punished (3:1–4). Thus the Old Testament's long quest of wisdom arrived, but tragically the answer of the Alexandrian Jew never gained entrance to the Bible of his countrymen in Palestine.

Although some Psalms may be classified with the Wisdom literature, the Psalter as such is far broader in character. The Psalms are Hebrew poetry. The title Psalter derives from the Greek word for stringed instrument or lyre. The word psalm means a hymn sung to the accompaniment of such a musical instrument. There are 150 psalms in the Bible. They are divided into five books or sections. The reader may notice that the same psalm is repeated in different books, for example, Psalm 13(14) is the same as Psalm 52(53).[2] Critical study has shown that partial collections existed at first. The reader should consider the Psalter as an anthology of the inspired poetry of Israel.

As Solomon was looked upon as the father of Hebrew wisdom, David was considered the father of Hebrew poetry. The Psalter came to be popularly called the Davidic Psalter. This should not be taken to mean that David is author of the entire Psalter. In the Hebrew Bible 73 Psalms bear the title "by [for] David"; 84 in the Greek version. There are certain critical questions concerning the meaning and value of these titles, but it is generally agreed that there was a Davidic collection of psalms, which is substantially preserved in the Psalter. Other Psalms are attributed to Asaph (12), to the sons of Core (11), and one each to Heman, to Ethan, to Moses and to Solomon. The

[2] The numbering of the Psalms differs in the Hebrew Bible and the versions due to different divisions of certain Psalms. The content is the same; only the numbering differs. The numbers in parenthesis are the King James numbering.

question of the origin and history of the Psalter is a complex critical question which scholars are freshly investigating. It may be said in a general way that it comprises several collections of psalms dating over a period of centuries beginning with David and extending to the period of the Second Temple.

It seems that poetry is man's oldest form of literary expression. Very old poetic fragments are preserved in the Old Testament in the sword song of Lamech (Gen. 4:23 f.) and in Josue's command to the sun (Jos. 10:12 f.), as well as the Song of Debora (Judges 5:2–31). Old poems in a complete state are the blessing of Jacob (Gen. 49:1–27), Moses' hymn of triumph (Ex. 15:1–18), the prayer of Anna (1 Sam. 2:1–10), David's lament over Saul and Jonathan (2 Sam. 1:18–27). The poetry of Israel was undoubtedly influenced by that of her neighbors. This is particularly true in the case of the Canaanites as demonstrated by the literature discovered as Ras Shamra. The impressive similarities of the Egyptian hymn of Akhenaten to Psalm 103 (104) have long been recognized. These comparisons do not prove a dependence of Hebrew poetry on that of Egypt or Ugarit, but the biblical genre is better understood when seen in this context. The most recent analogies come from the discovery of the Thanksgiving Psalms at Qumran.

As one might expect, the imagery of Hebrew poetry is Oriental. This will seem at times remote to our Western minds. Take for example the image in 113 A (114):4 that describes the trembling of the earth on the occasion of the theophany at Sinai:

> The mountains skipped like rams,
> and the hills like lambs of the flock.

The feeling and outlook is that of the ancient Orient. Moreover, the ethical attitudes are not those of a Christian. Observe the closing lines of the beautiful and nostalgic Psalm 136(137):

> O daughter of Babylon, you destroyer,
> . . . . . . . . . . . . . . . . . .
> Happy the man who shall seize and smash
> your little ones against the rock!

This is the feeling behind the law of talion, "An eye for an eye and a tooth for a tooth." It is not the feeling behind the Sermon on the Mount. This same spirit is expressed in the so-called imprecatory Psalms, which seem to imprecate evil upon an enemy. The classic example is Psalm 108 (109):

> May his children be fatherless,
> and his wife a widow.
> May his children be roaming vagrants and beggars,
> may they be cast out of the ruins of their homes.
> . . . . . . . . . . . . . . . . .
> May there be no one to do him kindness,
> nor anyone to pity his orphans. (9–12)

Such sentiments are offensive to the Christian conscience. They fit with Jesus' description of the Law: "You have heard that it was said, 'Thou shalt love thy neighbor and shalt hate thy enemy'" (Matt. 5:43). The Christian spirit is "Love your enemies, do good to those who hate you, and pray for those who persecute and calumniate you" (*ibid.*). Nothing brings out more forcibly the contrast of the two spirits. The reader must not forget that the Old Testament is not the New Testament, that the fullness of revelation came with Jesus, especially the revelation of the primacy of love and its universal extent. The Psalms, then, are set generally speaking in the same doctrinal frame as the Wisdom literature. These observations are not intended to detract from the greatness of the Psalter. They are designed rather to point out the limits of its spiritual horizons, to allay the reader's anxiety, or to help his perplexity.

In reading the Psalms it will serve the reader to know that they may be classified according to various genres. Recent study has explored the genres of the Psalter to good effect. The most we can do here is give some examples of this. For thorough study the reader must refer to commentaries on the Psalms.

A good example of the *hymn* genre is Psalm 103(104). It illustrates the fixed form of this genre: the introduction is an exhortation to praise God, which is often resumed in the conclusion. See verses 1 and 35: Bless the Lord, O my soul! The body of the poem gives the motives for praise, here the glorious works of creation. Praise is the characteristic note of the hymn genre. The center of interest is God. The song embodies disinterested praise. Psalm 103 is a fine example of lyrical religious poetry. Other Psalms in this genre are 8 (God's goodness to man), 18(19) (God's glory in the heavens and in the Law), 28(29) (God's majesty in the storm); 45(46) and 47(48) (chants of Sion, exalting Jerusalem as the city of the Most High God); 46(47), 92(93), 95(96), 97(98) (psalms of the kingdom of God marked by the language and imagery of the prophets).

Psalm 129(130), the familiar and favorite "De Profundis," is an example of the *supplication* genre. These psalms open with an appeal to God for help and close with a prayer, an expression of hope, or even an act of thanksgiving. In the development of the theme in the body of the psalm the speaker strives to move God to hear by rhetorical descriptions of his distress, of the enemies that surround him; he appeals to God's power and his goodness in the past. Some of these psalms are to be understood in a collective sense: that is, the nation laments on occasion of disaster, as in Psalm 43(44); or in an individual sense— for example, Psalm 21(22). The characteristic style is seen in Psalms 21(22) and 68(69).

Be not far from me, for I am in distress;
be near, for I have no one to help me.

Many bullocks surround me;
    the strong bulls of Basan encircle me. (21:12 f.)

Save me, O God,
    for the waters threaten my life;
I am sunk in the abysmal swamp
    where there is no foothold.
I have reached the watery depths;
    the flood overwhelms me. (68:2–3)

*Thanksgiving psalms* are similar to the hymn genre in their structure. The introduction often has the same ring as that of the hymn, the conclusion looks to the future with a promise to praise God, an invitation to the community to join the praise, or a blessing. The body of the psalm is narrative in form recalling the dangers endured or the enemies overcome. The heart of the psalm is the consecration of the victory by proclaiming God's power. A good example of this genre is Psalm 29(30):

Introduction:    2 I will extol you, O Lord, for you drew me clear and did not let my enemies rejoice over me.

Narrative:    3 O Lord, my God,
    I cried out to you and you healed me.
    O Lord, you brought me up from the nether world;
    You preserved me from among those going down into the pit.

. . . . . . . . . . . . . . . .

Conclusion:      12  You changed my mourning into danc-
                          ing;
                      You took off my sackcloth and clothed
                          me with gladness,
                      That my soul might sing praise to you
                          without ceasing;
                      O Lord, my God, forever will I give
                          thanks.

In discussing royal Messianism in Chapter Six we
quoted Psalms 2 and 88. *Royal psalms* such as these do
not constitute a distinct genre, but because of the importance of their subject they merit to be studied separately.
They are of two kinds, those that celebrate the kingship
of Yahweh, (46[47]; 92[93]–99[100]), and those that
celebrate the king of Israel. Basic to the latter is the concept of kingship in Israel discussed in Chapter Six. The
well-known Psalms 2, 44(45), and 109(110) pertain to
this class of royal psalms. They date from the period of
the monarchy and reflect the language and ceremonial of
the court.

The Messianic hope of Israel was forged to the dynasty
of David, and these Psalms were very likely first understood in a dynastic sense. With the development of Old
Testament Messianism they came to be understood of an
individual Messias. In the New Testament they are referred to Christ. Some of the psalms of the kingdom of
Yahweh are referred to the kingdom of Christ. Old Testa-

ment texts that are said to be fulfilled in Christ may be fulfilled in the literal sense or the typical sense. Christ fulfills a text in its literal sense when the words refer to him directly. He fulfills a text in the typical sense when the words of the text refer directly to a person who is a figure of Christ, for example, King David. Exegetes debate precisely how certain Old Testament texts are fulfilled in Christ, which depends upon their precise literal sense in the Old Testament.

A recent direction in interpreting the Psalms has been the effort to place them in a cult setting. These critics associate the royal psalms with a feast of the enthronement of Yahweh analogous to the enthronement of Marduk in Babylon. The existence of such a feast in Israel has not been established, and the idea has not won acceptance. Undoubtedly many Psalms had a liturgical setting in the Temple of Solomon, as well as in the Second Temple. They have a liturgical setting in the Church, heir to the Temple. In the breviary each Psalm is referred to the triune God by the addition of the doxology. The antiphons indicate the Christian motif that is to dominate its recitation. Thus in Matins of Pentecost the antiphon for Psalm 103 (104) is verse 30 (according to the Vulgate).

> Send forth thy Spirit
>    and they shall be created
> And thou shalt renew the face of the earth.

The title Canticle of Canticles (Song of Songs) is a Hebraism and means *the* Song, the song par excellence. The poem reads as a love song, and some have wondered why it is in the Bible. Two interpretations have been proposed. One affirms that the poem is an allegory describing figuratively the love of Yahweh for Israel and Israel's love of Yahweh. This was the interpretation of the rabbis. It was taken up by the Church Fathers, but became the love of Christ and his Church. The other interpretation affirms that it is what it seems: a love song. It is an inspired expression of the beauty and blessedness of human love and marriage, which is one of God's gifts.

Whatever be the literal meaning of the poem, it is aptly applied to describe the union of Christ and his Church, or Christ's union with the devout soul. Thus it was a favorite of the mystics, notably John of the Cross.

# TEN

# THE GOSPEL AND THE GOSPELS

The Old Testament was the Bible of the early Christian community until it produced books of its own that were considered to be inspired. It is noteworthy that the founder of Christianity left nothing in writing, particularly in view of his incomparable influence on human history. The only record we have of Jesus writing is in John 8:6: "Jesus, stooping down, began to write with his finger on the ground." The letters he wrote lasted until trodden on by some passer-by. Nor did Jesus commission his Apostles to write. He commissioned them to preach, as Peter testified in Acts 10:42—"he charged us to preach to the people." The mission of the Apostles, like that of the Master, was a mission of preaching. It is important to recognize this fact, since it is basic to understanding the relationship between the New Testament and the Church. The Church existed before the New Testament, produced the New Testament, and by virtue of her authority it was accepted as Scripture. It is because of this logic of history that the Church considers herself the authoritative interpreter of Scripture.

The whole matter swings on the hinge of authority. When Jesus came "preaching the gospel of the kingdom of God" (Mark 1:14) the religious authority of his people was Moses, as expressed primarily in the Torah (Law), the first five books of the Old Testament. The Jews were the people of the Book. They called the Old Testament "the Law and the Prophets." The books of "the Law and the Prophets" were just about identical with the Old Testament of the Jews of today.

A fact that emerges almost immediately one begins to read the record of the life of Jesus in the Gospels is that he presented himself as an authority superior to Moses. Nowhere is this seen more dramatically than in the Sermon on the Mount (Matt. 5–7). Jesus said, "You have heard that it was said to the ancients, 'Thou shalt not swear falsely, but fulfill thy oaths to the Lord.'" The reference is to the Torah, Leviticus 19:12 and Numbers 30:3. His listeners came to know the Law by hearing it read in the synagogue. Jesus proceeded to say, "But I say to you not to swear at all." Well does Matthew remark that the crowds were astonished because he taught "as one having authority" (7:29).

Jesus imparted his authority to his Apostles before he departed this earth. "All power in heaven and on earth has been given to me. Go, therefore, and make disciples of all nations, baptizing them in the name of the Father, and of the Son, and of the Holy Spirit, teaching them to observe all that I have commanded you; and behold, I am with you all days, even to the consummation of the world" (Matt. 28:18–20). They exercised this power (cf. Acts 4:18 ff.) while they lived. After their death their authority survived in their writings. This can be readily seen in the case of St. Paul's epistles. His letters bore his apostolic authority while he lived. Should they lose it at his death! What we call the Gospel of St. Mark was considered the preaching of St. Peter, as Clement and others testify. In fact its early title was "The Memoirs of Peter."

Since the Apostles were commissioned to preach, we might expect that there was a period of some duration during which the message of Christ existed only in oral form and only in the memories of living witnesses. We would very much like to know precisely what forms the preached Gospel assumed. Brief examples fortunately survive in the Acts of the Apostles (Acts 10:34–43). The four canonical Gospels are undoubtedly related to these primitive oral forms of preaching. In fact the study of the

Gospels under this aspect has been a very interesting phase of recent New Testament research. The method is termed Form Criticism (from the German, quite untranslatable, *Formgeschichte*), and endeavors to discover the more primitive sub-literary forms that lie behind the narratives and discourses of the Gospels.

The method as such is specifically a matter of literary criticism, but those who introduced it were set on finding the "historical" Christ. The Gospel picture of Christ was attributed to the creative faith of the primitive Christian community that transformed the man Christ into a divine being. Despite these unhappy associations, the literary method is recognized as having value and contributing to a deeper understanding of the nature of the Gospels. Contemporary Catholic scholars assert that the Gospels reflect the faith of the Christian community. They are a witness to that faith. For them the creative force is not the Christian community that altered the Christ of history, but the historical Christ who formed the faith of the community. The emphasis at the moment has shifted from the study of forms to the question of editing (*Redaktionsgeschichte*) —that is, the use made of the forms by the Evangelists.

A much more dramatic shift is seen in Prof. Rudolf Bultmann, who moved on from Form Criticism to demythologizing (*Demytholozierung*). Two notions are basic to Bultmann's approach: mythology and existentialism. He considers everything in the New Testament a "mythical" expression of "authentic existence." The myth presents the invisible and the divine in terms of human and visible, namely, the redemptive death of Jesus and his resurrection. This, says Bultmann, is unacceptable to the modern mind. There is, however, underlying the mythical language authentic existence. For Bultmann only the death of Christ on the cross is historical, and must be interpreted in existentialist terms. Salvation consists in the encounter of the individual with the death of Christ, which was a lesson for all mankind. Faith denuded of myth means to interpret our human existence authentically, that is, in terms of divine and invisible realities, as opposed to the false security of the world. Demythologizing is the current style in liberal German theology, the latest in a long succession. It has been criticized by non-Catholic as well as Catholic scholars as arbitrary and a false direction in New Testament studies, belonging to the area of psychoanalysis and philosophy rather than biblical exegesis.

Contemporary Catholic work in New Testament studies is influenced by the method of Form Criticism and literary genres. The Church's scholars are interested in determining to what extent the interpretation of the Christian community is reflected in the texts, the premise being that the Synoptics as well as John show evidence of theological reflection. The influence of the liturgy on the formation of the Gospels is also receiving attention; and of course the Qumran manuscripts are being carefully studied. They throw light on the cultural background of the New Testament writings, particularly on John and Paul. New Testament eschatology is likewise being reviewed. Indeed research has entered a very active phase. These things sooner or later affect the common reader in some degree.

When the early Christian heard the word gospel he did not think of a written record of the sayings and the deeds of Jesus; to him the word meant the good tidings (*euaggelion*) of salvation through Christ, the message of redemption. He did not think of four Gospels. The Gospel was one. When written Gospels made their appearance they were titled "the Gospel according to Matthew" or simply "according to Mark." Gospel first meant the living word of preaching and only later referred to writing.

Can we reconstruct the history that lies between the preached Gospel and our four written Gospels? It can be done with only a measure of certainty and a large portion of conjecture. We are sure that the Gospel existed first in oral form, and it is likely that the oral form soon took on a definitive pattern or plan, or perhaps several patterns, according to the region where it was preached; for example to Jews in Jerusalem or Greeks in Alexandria. Peter's sermon in Acts 10:34–43 may serve as an example of the primitive oral catechesis. Observe the outline of the sermon: 1) the preaching of the Baptist and the Baptism of Jesus; 2) the Galilean ministry; 3) the passing from Galilee to Judea and Jerusalem; 4) the Passion, death, and Resurrection. It is interesting that we find the same plan in the Gospel of St. Mark. Now a very early witness, Papias, Bishop of Hierapolis, affirms about 130 A.D. that

"Mark, having been the interpreter of Peter, wrote down carefully, though not in order, all that he remembered, both words and deeds of the Lord . . . he took care to omit or falsify nothing which he had heard [from Peter]." The correlation of these texts suggests an intimate link between the preaching of Peter and the written Mark.

Of course this is only the barest outline of the story. Can we fill in the details? To do so we must bring in the Gospels of Matthew and Luke. They reveal the same basic plan as Mark. This takes on greater significance when they are compared with John, who has a different plan. The first three Gospels not only have the same general plan; they have striking similarities in the order of individual events, and at times they have verbatim identity. We may arrange the data of the three Gospels in parallel columns to see them at one glance (*sunopsis*). This is the reason they are called the Synoptic Gospels. The relationship between them has been described as *concordia discors*. It is certain that there is an interrelationship between these three in the written forms. The exact nature of this relationship is differently explained.

It is certain that the Gospels are a compilation; they are mosaics composed of bits and pieces that existed separately, such as healing narratives or Passion narratives. This fact emerges from a study of the Gospels and the method of Form Criticism has confirmed it. In the prologue to his Gospel, Luke says that "many have undertaken to draw up a narrative concerning the things that have been fulfilled among us" (1:1). He then declares his intention to write "an orderly account" (1:3). Among the "many" accounts that Luke refers to were undoubtedly Matthew and Mark, since Luke wrote later. It is not likely that all the accounts were complete and orderly. The story thus reconstructed suggests: 1) the preached Gospel, 2) the separate narratives or forms, and 3) the compilation of these in the three Gospels as we know them.

A comparison of Mark with the other Synoptics reveals that of Mark's 673 verses more than 600 are found in Matthew in substance, and about 350 of them in Luke. It reveals that the order of Mark is generally found in Matthew and Luke, and the same may be said for the majority of Mark's Greek words. The most significant difference between Mark and the other two is in relating the words of Jesus. Matthew's Gospel is built on the plan of five discourses; the first and most familiar, the Sermon on the Mount. There is a similar discourse in Luke, but not in Mark. We may therefore distinguish in the Gospels the *narratives* and the *discourses* (what Jesus *did* and what Jesus *said*), and this distinction is critical in understanding what follows.

Christian tradition from the earliest times held the Apostle Matthew to be the author of the first Gospel in its original Aramaic form. This is clearly stated by Origen in the first half of the third century. "The Gospel according to Matthew, who was first a publican and later the Apostle of Jesus Christ, was the first to be written; it was

written in the Hebrew [Aramaic] language for the believers from Judaism." This tradition was unchallenged
until the eighteenth-century enlightenment and the nine-
teenth-century criticism. Since then Christian scholars are
divided on the question. In 1911 Rome's Biblical Commission considered the question of sufficient moment to
issue directives on it to this effect: The Apostle Matthew
is truly author of the Gospel that bears his name; he wrote
first and in Aramaic; the Greek Matthew is substantially
identical with the Aramaic original; it may not be "held
as probable" that Matthew composed "only a collection of
sayings and discourses."

This last reference is to the theory of non-Catholic critics
who held the so-called Two Source Theory. This proposed
that canonical Mark is the earliest Gospel, that Matthew
is later, that it depends upon Mark in its narrative sections
and upon another source for its discourses. This "sayings
source" is entitled Q, the first letter of the German word
for source, *Quelle*. This became the dominant hypothesis
of non-Catholic scholarship. It has been seriously chal-
lenged by some recent writers, notably the non-Catholic
Pierson Parker in *The Gospel before Mark*, Abbot Butler
of Downside in *The Originality of St. Matthew,* and Professor Vaganay in *Le Problème Synoptique*.

Some contemporary Catholic scholars propose opinions
that combine elements of the traditional and the critical
positions. This new direction is attributable to the critical
research of the decades that intervene since the directives

of the Commission and to a change in the intellectual climate. What may be called a Catholic Two Source Theory is proposed by Alfred Wickenhauser, professor emeritus of New Testament literature at the University of Freiburg: Mark is the oldest Gospel composed in Greek; canonical Greek Matthew depends on Mark, as does Luke, in the narrative sections. The common source (Q) of Matthew and Luke consisted principally of discourse material; the author of Q is the Apostle Matthew; it was a sayings source in Aramaic, substantially identical with our canonical Matthew (*New Testament Introduction*, pp. 249 ff.).

The Gospels as we know them are the end term of a process. By means of the external witness of history and the science of literary criticism, scholars reconstruct the story of their origin and development with some certainty and much conjecture. It is an accepted tenet of New Testament scholarship that the Gospels are kerugmatic in character, that is, they reflect the apostolic preaching (Greek: *kerugma*) of what Jesus "did" and what he "taught" (Acts 1:1). The Gospels therefore should not be looked upon as a biography of Jesus in the modern use of that term. They are a statement of the faith of the Christian community founded on the historical fact of Jesus and preached to the world. The final forms of the Gospels depend upon their individual authors, each of whom wrote for a specific purpose. It may help the reader to think of them as editors or redactors in view of what has been said just above. This aspect of the matter is important to the common reader for understanding the message of the Gospels. It is in the redaction that divine inspiration is certainly involved, whatever may be said about the inspiration of the earlier sub-literary forms.

The observations on the Synoptic question manifest that the same ground plan is common to Matthew, Mark, and Luke. It is this: At first the crowds receive Jesus favorably; but the humble and spiritual Messianism of Jesus is contrary to their expectations and they are disenchanted; Jesus withdraws from Galilee and forms about himself a small group of loyal disciples; at Caesarea Phillipi he wins their absolute commitment. This moment is decisive; the movement is then toward Jerusalem, where the climax of the drama is enacted in the increased opposition that led to his Passion and death; the final act is the response of God in the triumph of Christ's Resurrection. The dominant idea that is common to the first three Gospels is the paradox of Jesus. Each one treats it with his own specific emphasis.

With Mark the essential theme is the paradox of a crucified Messias. He presents Jesus as the Son of God (1:1), acknowledged as such by the Father (1:11), conscious of his divine Messiaship from the powers he exercised (2:10, forgiveness of sins) and his miracles. In contrast to this, Mark strongly depicts the apparent check on Jesus from the opposition of men which leads to his crucifixion. It is the scandal of the Cross that Mark is preoccupied to explain. This he does by opposing to it the triumph of the Resurrection and the fact that it was so because of the mysterious plan of God. According to this divine plan mankind would be redeemed by the death of the Suffering Messias. This ran counter to Jewish expectations of nationalistic and materialistic Messianism. Therefore Jesus withdrew and avoided public acclaim. This behavior of Jesus has been described as the "Messianic secret," and it receives particular emphasis in Mark.

The emphasis in Matthew is on the "kingdom of heaven." The very expression suggests the Aramaic background of the Gospel, since "heaven" is a substitute for "God," in keeping with the custom of the Jews who abstained from uttering the divine name. The notable structural difference of Matthew from Mark is the inclusion of five long discourses: a statement of the program of the kingdom in the Sermon on the Mount (5–7); instruction to the disciples who are to preach the kingdom (10); the mysterious nature of the kingdom is described in parables (13); the duties of the disciples of the kingdom (18); the eschatological phase of the kingdom (24–25). The narrative portions are subordinated to discourses, serving as introductions to them. Matthew also adds the infancy narratives.

A notable feature of Matthew is his use of the Old Testament. The kingdom of God preached by Jesus was announced in the Old Testament, and Matthew is particularly interested in demonstrating for his Jewish readers that in the person and the work of Jesus the Scriptures are fulfilled. For this reason he quotes the Old Testament frequently. His Gospel is the charter of the new economy in which God's designs are fulfilled. Christ is the fulfillment of the kingdom of God in the Old Testament, not only in the sense that he realizes in himself the Messianic predictions, but that the "Law and the Prophets" are brought to that perfection which is the regime of love.

Luke follows the plan of Mark with some alterations, omissions, and one notable addition (9:51–18:14). Comparative study of the third Gospel with Matthew and Mark reveals the delicate sensitivity of Luke in handling his sources. The key concepts are the same as those of Matthew and Mark but critics detect the influence of Paul on Luke's personal religious psychology. His Gospel has been described as the Gospel of the women, particularly of the Mother of Jesus; the Gospel of prayer; the Gospel of mercy; the Gospel of joy. All these titles are valid. Luke also reveals a predilection for the Holy City and for the Holy Spirit.

The fourth Gospel, that of John, differs from the Synoptic Gospels in structure, content, and dominant idea. The structure of the Synoptics, as we have seen above, is built essentially around the Galilean ministry of Jesus. The Judean and Jerusalem ministry is central to the fourth Gospel. The Synoptics bring Jesus to Jerusalem for the Passover of the Passion, giving the impression of a short public ministry of one year; John clearly indicates three Paschs, suggesting a ministry of at least two years. Narrative sections in John are for the most part different from those of the Synoptics. John includes discourses, but they are not the discourses of Matthew or of Luke. They differ both in content and style. Most critics believe that John knew the Synoptics, and some propose that his purpose was to supplement them. Most agree that there is no literary dependence of John on the Synoptics, but that he presents an independent and original witness to the primitive Christian catechesis. Recent research has substantiated the historical value of the fourth Gospel.

The dominant concept of the fourth Gospel is expressed in 20:31. "These [things] are written that you may believe that Jesus is the Christ [Messias], the Son of God, and that believing you may have life in his name." John presents the mystery of the Incarnation in relation to the mystery of life in Christ. In the fourth Gospel "eternal life" corresponds to "the kingdom" of the Synoptics. In these the "glory" of Christ is to be revealed particularly in his Second Coming; in John eschatology is already realized in the "coming" of the Incarnation, the Cross, the Resurrection, and the indwelling of the Holy Spirit. "Now is the judgment of the world," John affirms (12:31); the consummation of the kingdom and the ultimate victory of God over evil will come with the Parousia, that is, the "Presence" (of the Lord). In John "eternal life" is a reality of the present world; in the Synoptics it is eschatological, that is, associated with "the last things" (Greek: *eschata*).

The plan of the fourth Gospel would seem to be determined by the *kerugma* and the liturgy. The Jewish feasts provide its structure: three Passovers (2:13; 6:4; 11:55), an unnamed feast (5:1), a Feast of Tabernacles (7:2), a Feast of the Dedication (10:22). The feasts do more than provide a structure for the deeds and discourses of Jesus. They are related to their meaning. Observe how the Feast of Tabernacles (Booths) provides the unifying theme of the section 7:1–10:21. During the seven days of feast the people dwelt in booths made of branches, reminiscent of their forefathers who dwelt in tents in the desert. Daily during the feast a priest filled a golden vessel with water from the pool of Siloam and carried it to the Temple, where it was received with a trumpet blast. Mixed with the sacrificial wine it was poured out at the altar. It was also the custom in the evening to illuminate the Court of the Women from two high stands bearing four immense lamps that cast light over much of the city. Note how this liturgical context gives meaning to Jesus' words in 7:37 ff., "If anyone thirst, let him come to me and drink. He who believes in me, as the Scripture says, 'From within him there shall flow rivers of living water.'" He said this, however, of the Spirit those who believed in him were to receive; and in 8:12, "I am the light of the world. He who follows me does not walk in darkness, but will have the light of life." Is John suggesting in this that the Jewish institutions come to an end in their fulfillment in Christ?

The fourth Gospel is strongly marked by symbolism. It is not a symbolism that replaces facts, but one that flows from the events. John chooses events in the life of Jesus that have symbolic meaning, thus illustrating the spiritual meaning of Christ. The miracles of the fourth Gospel are "signs" in this sense. The cure of the blind man (9:1–4) is symbolic of Jesus as the Light of the World and of the blindness of his foes. The resurrection of Lazarus (11:1–45) is symbolic of Jesus as the Resurrection and the Life. Recent research has detected a Christian liturgical and sacramental symbolism in John. The discourse with Nicodemus, for example, (3:1–21) contains elements of the Christian catechesis on Baptism. The entire Gospel is dominated by the idea that the Christian Pasch replaces the ancient Passover (see particularly 19:36). The purification rites of the Jews are replaced by the purification of the Spirit (20:22). The life of Jesus is therefore presented in relation to the Christian life in the sacramental mysteries.

The fourth Gospel is marked by certain antitheses, such as light-darkness, truth-error, good-evil. Recent discoveries at Wady Qumran have made known the literature of an Essenic sect whose terminology is closely related to the language of John. Some comparative studies have already been made by scholars, but for the present conclusions must be tentative. These discoveries have shifted the emphasis from Hellenism to Judaism in the question of influences on the fourth Gospel. As a result we realize that there is much we do not know about the Jewish world in the first century, and that it is advisable to proceed with caution. The Qumran scrolls, more familiarly called the Dead Sea Scrolls, reveal definite affinities of language and thought with the fourth Gospel. It is in this area that their significance lies rather than in undermining the originality of Christ and Christianity. They have thrown much light on the Jewish backgrounds of the New Testament, and further careful study will determine more precisely the character and measure of that influence.

# ELEVEN

# THE WORD AND WORK OF THE APOSTLES

The Acts of the Apostles is the second part of Luke's literary work. Taken together with the third Gospel the work may be described as "the history of Christian beginnings." The word Acts in the title is Middle English influenced by the *Acta* of the Latin title through the French *actes*. A preferable English equivalent of *praxeis* in the Greek title would be "deeds." The Greek title finds analogies in such ancient works as "The Deeds of Alexander" or "The Deeds of Hannibal." The Acts of the Apostles does not pretend to be a complete history of the primitive Christian community. Its concern is almost exclusively with the deeds of Peter and Paul. Nonetheless, it is an invaluable record of important aspects of the early Church: for example, Baptism in water and the Spirit (1:5); celebration of the Eucharist (2:42); beginnings of ecclesiastical organization (presbyters, 11:30); holding possessions in common (2:44).

The idea that dominates Acts is that the work of Christ did not end with his departure from this earth. From heaven the glorified Lord continues his work in his Apostles vested with power from on high; this through the establishing of his Church and the preaching of his Gospel throughout the world (cf. 1:8). It is the history of the universal sweep of Christianity across the world through the power of the Holy Spirit. Luke's particular interest is to show the transition of the Christian movement from the Jewish world to the larger Gentile world. This determines the selection and treatment of his source material. Thus he features the conversion of the Roman centurion Cornelius (10:1–11:18), the Gentile mission at Antioch (11:19–30). He devotes the second half of Acts to Paul's missionary journeys, since he was incontestably the greatest and the most successful of the Gentile missionaries.

The doctrinal teaching of Acts is of incalculable value as a record of the earliest Christian faith. This appears particularly in the discourses. We have already referred to Acts 10:34–43 as an example of the apostolic *kerugma*, a sort of précis of the Gospel of Mark. Peter's discourse in

Acts 2:14–36 shows the centrality of the resurrection of Christ to the apostolic catechesis and how Old Testament texts were employed to show that Jesus was the fulfillment of prophecy. Acts 17:22–31 preserves a supreme example of Paul's missionary discourses to a cultured pagan audience. Paul began soon after his conversion "to preach that Jesus is the Son of God" (9:20).

The crucial problem of the infant Church was the admission of Gentiles. Should they be obliged to circumcision and observance of the Mosaic Law? Converts from Judaism were already circumcised and observers of the Law. The tension appeared in the Jerusalem community between the group faithful to the Law, led by James, and the Hellenists with Stephen as their spokesman. The problem grew with the expansion of the Church into the Greek world, and it plagued Paul on his early missionary journeys. The existence of the problem must be known by the common reader in order to understand some of Paul's letters, particularly Galatians. Those called Judaizers insisted that in order to enter the Church, Gentiles must be circumcised and observe the Mosaic Law. They insisted that the Gentiles had to enter the Church by passing through the vestibule of Judaism. Paul contended that this was contrary to the very principle of Christianity, namely, that man is saved through faith in Jesus Christ. The question was settled at the Council of Jerusalem in A.D. 49, described in Acts 15. Paul's position supported by Peter was confirmed by the apostolic college.

The historical value of Acts is frequently confirmed by Paul's letters. The second section, 13–28, should be read in conjunction with his letters for fuller understanding and appreciation. Independent critics are less skeptical today about the historicity of Acts than an earlier generation. Accounts of miracles and the supernatural in Acts are quite acceptable to one who accepts the possibility of miracles. Supernatural events are related with great restraint by Luke. He does not write like an unreliable visionary.

In the New Testament there are twenty-one letters. About fourteen thousand letters have survived from antiquity, and some of them are original copies. As a rule letters were written on papyrus, usually only on one side. The papyrus was rolled up. When a longer roll was desired pieces of papyrus were joined end to end, and the large roll could be mounted on two spools. This would form a scroll. Letters were ordinarily dictated to a scribe, the sender adding his signature in his own hand. "I, Paul, greet you with my own hand. This is the mark in every letter. Thus I write" (2 Thess. 3:17). We are informed by Cicero and others that the scribe sometimes acted as secretary as well; that is, he would phrase the letter as well as write it. This throws some interesting light on questions of authenticity. If the scribe as secretary is responsible for the language and style, these would not be decisive in determining authorship. It has been suggested

that we are to understand 1 Peter 5:12 in this way: "*By*
Silvanus . . . I have written to you thus briefly."

Another observation that may serve the reader is to note
the distinction between a letter and an epistle. It is true
that we ordinarily use the term epistle, but actually Paul's
writings, with the exception of Hebrews, are better termed
letters. They conform to the accepted style as we know
it from antiquity, particularly from the many papyri discovered in Egypt. A letter is private, an epistle is public.
A letter is informal, an epistle is literary. An epistle is a
treatise in letter form, intended for a wide group or even
the world, such as the papal encyclicals (circulating
epistles). A letter is written to a particular person or group
on a definite occasion, for a definite purpose, and is intended for them alone. In this sense thirteen of Paul's
epistles are really letters. The "Catholic epistles" on the
other hand are more truly epistles.

The life of St. Paul is best learned directly from the
Acts and his letters. There one gets the real impression of
the dizzying heights of his achievement and feels the fire
of his overpowering mind and heart. Truly he was a man
who in God changed the face of the earth. Some lines of
his life can be underscored here to assist the reader. Paul's
Greek background is significant. Tarsus, his birthplace,
was famed as a center of Greek philosophy. He did not
receive a formal Greek education, but his active mind
learned much from his environment. He had the formal
rabbinical education with Gamaliel in Jerusalem. This is

significant for his exegetical method in using the Old Testament. He was an ardent Pharisee. He became a Christian probably in A.D. 34. Acts records three missionary journeys, the first beginning in 46 and the last terminating in A.D. 58. He founded churches throughout Turkey and Greece. He was imprisoned in Caesarea from 58 to 60 and in Rome from 61 to 63. Acts does not take us beyond this point in his life, but old traditions say he was later released and journeyed again to the East and to Spain. He died in the persecution of Nero, probably in A.D. 67.

In taking up the letters it is preferable to read them in the order of their appearance rather than the order in which they are found in our Bible. That order apparently was determined on the basis of dignity—first of churches, Rome, Corinth, Galatia, and so on; then of persons, Timothy, Titus, Philemon. Critics are in general agreement on the chronological order of the letters, with some difference of opinion concerning the position of Galatians. The editors of the *Westminster Version of the Sacred Scriptures* adopt the chronological arrangement of the letters of St. Paul. This does contribute to the reader's understanding of the letters and also serves to bring out the development of Paul's thought. For the rest, in this brief exposition we can only give some indication of Paul's key ideas and some illustration of his exegetical method, colored as it was by his rabbinical training.

The letters of Paul were written between the years 50 and 67, the date of his death. When the first letters were written, the Church was just twenty years old. If the

Gospel of Mark was written in the middle or late fifties, Paul's first epistles would be the earliest written witness to the Christian faith. The first in order of time were the two epistles to the Thessalonians written during the winter of 50–51 A.D. Thessalonica is present day Salonica. The Apostle founded the church there in the course of his second missionary journey (Acts 17:1–9).

The central theme of these epistles is the Second Coming of the Lord. They are the earliest statement of Christian teaching on eschatology. The Parousia was very prominent in the consciousness of the first Christians. We may gather from these letters that it received special emphasis in the early phase of Paul's preaching. In any event the new converts of Thessalonica were concerned about the lot of the departed at the glorious coming of Christ. In his first letter the Apostle reassures them that the living will not be favored over the dead (4:15). The Apostle's teaching on the Second Coming of Christ is described in colors of the apocalyptic tradition in the Jewish and Christian communities. The reader may consult for sake of comparison the eschatological discourse of Jesus as reported in the Synoptics, particularly in Matthew 24. The Church emphasizes the timelessness of the doctrine of the Parousia by reading 1 Thessalonians 4:13–18 in the Requiem Mass of the day of death or burial.

The second epistle followed shortly after the first, occasioned by the anxiety of the community that the Day of the Lord was imminent. The preachers of the doctrine appealed among other things to a real or purported letter of Paul. This led the Apostle to emphasize the fact that certain events must precede the Parousia, namely, the religious apostasy and the appearance of the "man of sin." This would be the Antichrist, although Paul does not use the term. The teaching in this place is incomplete, since the Apostle presumes certain points to be familiar to them from the oral catechesis. Thus the force or person "restraining" the "mystery of iniquity" cannot be identified with certainty (2:5 ff.). One suggestion is that the obstacle is the preaching of the Gospel.

There is some uncertainty as we have already indicated concerning the date of the Epistle to the Galatians. Some critics consider it the first of Paul's letters and place it prior to the Council of Jerusalem (A.D. 49). Others judge it to be later, about the year 57. Critical opinion is also divided on the destination of the letter. Some critics favor the churches of South Galatia, others those of North Galatia. These questions are rather technical in character, and the division of opinion is due to different interpretations of key texts in Acts and Galatians. What will be immediately obvious to the reader is that the letter was written under great emotional stress. The reasoning bends under the weight of emotions. Sentences go unfinished, transitions are abrupt, the language is vehement. It is important for the reader to know the cause of Paul's emotional disturbance. It was the activity of the Judaizers among his Galatian converts.

The Judaizing crisis, to which we have referred above,

had to do with the question of justification and salvation. Fortunately the Apostle treated the question again, this time calmly, in the Epistle to the Romans, written shortly after Galatians. Thus the obscurities of Galatians can be clarified by consulting Romans. At the heart of the conflict was the question of the Mosaic Law and circumcision. The Judaizers insisted that no man could be saved without circumcision and observance of the Law. Paul argued that the Law was provisory and temporary, and that the grace promised to Abraham before the Law came into existence is given through Christ. Christ's redeeming death and justifying resurrection mark the termination of the Law. Through Christ and in Christ man receives gratuitously a "justice of God" (Rom. 10:3).[1] Under the Law man strove to justify himself by performing the works of the Law, which were powerless in themselves to justify. To demand that Christians return to the Law would be to make void the Cross of Christ. The question was of fundamental importance to Christianity and the world. Paul saw it basically as a question of freedom or slavery. Since the question has theological relevance, note carefully that Paul contrasts "faith" to "the works *of the Law*." To extend the meaning of "works" beyond that is to go beyond Paul's meaning and without Paul's support.

A comparison of the following texts may serve as an illustration of the relationship existing between Galatians

---

[1] Justification is a divine grace, which transforms us completely within. It comes from God and is related to his "justice" as merciful, faithful, and vindicator of the sovereign good.

and Romans and also of the nature of Paul's argument from Scripture. The Judaizers argued that men must become children of Abraham by circumcision in order to share in the blessings promised to him. Paul did not deny that men must become children of Abraham; he did deny that circumcision was necessary for that. He asserted that Abraham was justified by his faith (Gen. 15:6) *before* he was circumcised (Gen. 17:9–14). Therefore faith identified men with Abraham, circumcised or not. (Emphasis supplied.)

### Galatians 3:6–9

It is just as with Abraham, who *believed* God, and it was accounted to him for justification. Understand, then, that those whose reliance springs from *faith*, they are the sons of Abraham. And the Scripture, foreseeing that God would *justify* the Gentiles by means of *faith*, announced this good news beforehand to Abraham, "In thee shall all the nations be blessed." So then, those who spring from *faith* are blessed with faithful Abraham.

### Romans 4:9–12

We were saying [4:3] that to Abraham his *faith* was counted *for justification*. How then was it so counted? *After* he was circumcised, or *before* he was circumcised? *Not after* he was circumcised, but *before* he was circumcised. And he received circumcision as a token, a seal of the *justification* arising from his *faith*, while he was *uncircumcised*, in order that he might be the father of *all* the *uncircumcised believers*—that justification might be counted to them also— and the father of circumcision to those who not only are of the circumcision, but who also walk in the steps of *that faith* which our father Abraham had while he was yet uncircumcised.

Galatians is an expression of Paul's Gospel of freedom from the Law in a specific historical situation. Romans is a reasoned vindication of the fundamental principle that justification is effected by faith without the works of the Mosaic Law. This is the main argument of Romans, not the only one. In 9–11 the Apostle addresses himself to the difficult question of Israel's rejection. The Apostle declares that God has suffered their blindness to permit the Gentile nations to enter the kingdom of God. Their rejection was not total since some believed; nor is it final, since one day Israel will return, for God is faithful to his promises. The epistle is the oldest and most reliable evidence we possess regarding the Christian community in Rome, and by contrast contains Paul's celebrated description of the moral corruption of the pagan world (1:18–23).

The description of pagan immorality may have been suggested by the city of Corinth, where Paul wrote the epistle to the Romans. Men verbalized Corinth—it meant to play the libertine. Corinth was a port city, a motley medley of men and of gods. There were Romans, Jews, and Greeks, and Orientals. There was Jupiter from Rome, Artemis from Ephesus, and Isis from Egypt. The temple of Aphrodite in old Corinth had more than a thousand temple prostitutes. Paul came to this city in A.D. 50 preaching Christ crucified, and *mirabile dictu* he soon had a flourishing Christian community there.

The two letters to the Corinthians were written around the year 57. Critical questions connected with the letters are rather complex. In 1 Corinthians 5:9 the Apostle refers to a letter he wrote. This "pre-canonical" letter is partially preserved in 2 Corinthians 6:14–7:1 according to some critics. In 2 Corinthians 2:4 Paul refers to a letter he wrote "with many tears." Some see a part of this letter in 2 Corinthians 10–13. The reader may easily observe that 7:2 seems to be the logical continuity of 6:13, thus suggesting that 6:14–7:1 is an insert. Scholars have observed the striking literary affinity between this section and the documents from Qumran. There is some uncertainty, too, in reconstructing the history of Paul's personal contacts with the community around this time. These brief notes are set down only to familiarize the reader with the fact that the letters pose several critical problems. For fuller study he must turn to works of biblical introduction or commentaries.

The two letters reveal much of Paul's personality and the extent of his work (1 Cor. 9; 2 Cor. 10–12). They are a revealing chiaroscuro of the moral and religious life of a segment of the Greek world converted to Christ— factions, immorality, doctrinal difficulties. At Corinth people were saying that the Apostle lacked the polish of wisdom, the lofty concepts of the philosopher, and the rhetoric of the orator. This called forth Paul's telling exposition of the Christian wisdom (1 Cor. 2:1–16). "We speak the wisdom of God, mysterious, hidden" (2:7). In the section 7:1–15:18 of 1 Corinthians the Apostle replies to the questions asked concerning marriage and virginity, eating of idol's meats, abuses in liturgical assemblies (with the earliest account of the Lord's Supper), charisms (with the renowned hymn to charity in 13), the resurrection of the dead. The significance of the Apostle's replies is that his genius reduces these questions to doctrinal principles, such as the true liberty of the Christian life, the primacy of charity, the Mystical Body. The second epistle is mainly a defense of his apostolate in the face of the community and his opponents.

The four epistles just considered are termed the great epistles. The four we are about to consider are called the captivity epistles. They are Ephesians, Philippians, Colossians, and Philemon. The captivity referred to was traditionally understood as Paul's imprisonment in Rome from A.D. 61 to 63. The Roman origin of Philippians, supported universally by tradition, has been questioned by recent scholarship. On the basis of internal evidence the alternative view is advanced that it was written during an earlier imprisonment at Ephesus about A.D. 56/57. This imprisonment is conjectural, since it is nowhere mentioned. The arguments adduced to support it are worthy of consideration. It is popular among contemporary non-Catholic critics and has won some Catholic support, for example, Benoit and Gaechter. In this view Philippians would be associated with the great epistles rather than those of the Roman captivity.

There is also some critical question concerning the unity of the letter. Some find evidences of conflation of several letters, but it is almost impossible to prove it. The letter is more personal than doctrinal. Philippi was Paul's favorite community and the letter is an outpouring of his heart. The Apostle's appeal to unity and humility among his converts called forth the powerful description of Christ's humiliation in 2:6–11, words that serve so effectively the liturgy of Holy Week.

Colossians and Ephesians should be read together. They stand to each other in somewhat the same relationship as Galatians to Romans. Paul's authorship of Ephesians is seriously contested by independent critics because of its different language, style, and theological thought. Catholic critics do not deny these differences, but feel they can be sufficiently explained by the supposition that Paul commissioned a disciple to write it according to his ideas and plan. There is some obscurity in regard to the destination of the letter. The oldest and best manuscripts—for example, Papyrus 46 and Codex Vaticanus—do not have the reading "at Ephesus" in 1:1. The internal evidence of the letter itself does not suggest the community of Ephesus. It seems that the letter was a circular letter addressed to several churches of Asia Minor in the neighborhood of Ephesus, and that a space was left blank to be filled in according to place where it was read (cf. Col. 4:16). This would explain the impersonal tone of the letter.

From the doctrinal view both letters are eminently Christological. The error that occasioned their writing was a syncretism of Judaism and Gnosticism. From Gnosticism came the cosmological concept, a theory about "the elements of the world" (Col. 2:8). These were conceived as intermediate beings or angelic powers, in whom the *pleroma*, the "fullness of the Godhead," dwelt (cf. Col. 1:19). They were the cause of creation and since they exercised power over men, they had to be worshiped. The asceticism of the movement stemmed from the influence of Jewish legalism.

This error gave the Apostle the occasion to expound the cosmological aspect of the work of Christ, as distinguished from the soteriological, or the theology of salvation. The syncretism at Colossa carried an implicit denial of the *unique* position of Christ as Redeemer and Mediator. In two famous Christological passages (1:15–20 and 2:9–15) Paul demonstrates the pre-eminence of Christ above all cosmic powers. Christ has taken over their cosmic role. As they were subject to the pre-existent Son, so they are subject to the glorified Christ. In him dwells "the fullness of the Godhead bodily" (Col. 2:9). United to Christ, as members to the head of the Mystical Body, the Christians "have died to the elements of the world," they are released from their tyranny of superstitious rites. There can be no question that we encounter here an expansion of Paul's theology. Note, however, the continuity of this theology with his earlier thought. The roots of this Christology already appear in 1 Corinthians 8:6; 2 Corinthians 5:19; Galatians 4:4 f.; Romans 8:38 ff. This development of Pauline Christology has been aptly described as realized eschatology.

The same themes appear in the Epistle to the Ephesians. The dominating idea is the Church as universal and united to Christ. Many themes from the earlier letters are taken up again and woven into Paul's finest synthesis.

The short letter to Philemon was written at the same time. It is a touching example of the Christian behavior, brotherly love between a master and slave, in an un-Christian social setting. The same principle would in time undermine the institution of slavery itself.

The two epistles addressed to Timothy and the one addressed to Titus form the little group called the pastoral epistles. For the past century and a half they have borne the brunt of critical attack and the regnant thesis of liberal critics is that they are not Pauline. Catholic critics and conservative Protestant critics defend their authenticity. The latter feel that differences of language and style are sufficiently explained if the epistles were written by a disciple-secretary. St. Luke has been suggested for the role.

The three epistles are closely related in content and form. They have an official character and are therefore, properly speaking, epistles rather than letters, although 2 Timothy approaches the letter in character. The main concern of the pastorals is the exercise of the pastoral office, organization of the Church, and opposition to false teachings. First Timothy and Titus were probably written about the year 65, and 2 Timothy may be considered Paul's last will, written just before his death in A.D. 67.

## TWELVE

## LETTERS AND PROPHECY

The Epistle to the Hebrews has been beset by questions from the beginning. The questions are aimed at its canonicity as well as its authenticity. Canonicity means that it is divinely inspired—that it has God for its author. Authenticity means that it really proceeds from the human author to whom it is attributed. From the outset the epistle was received as canonical Scripture by the Eastern churches of Alexandria, Palestine, Syria, and Asia Minor. They also held it to be Pauline, recognizing withal that elsewhere the Pauline authorship was questioned. In the Western Church on the other hand it was not, with rare exceptions, received as canonical and Pauline until the middle of the fourth century. The African councils of Hippo (A.D. 393) and Carthage (A.D. 397) in listing the books of the New Testament canon say "thirteen epistles of Paul the Apostle, and one by the same to the Hebrews." The distinction is interesting and undoubtedly reflects the uncertainty regarding authenticity or canonicity. The Roman Synod of 382 lists fourteen epistles of Paul, as does the fourth Council of Carthage in 419.

The Council of Trent (1546) in a decree of faith fixed definitively the canon of Scripture. It listed the fourteen epistles of Paul by name. For Catholics, therefore, the canonicity of Hebrews is a doctrine of faith. It must be accepted as divinely inspired. This does not close the question of authenticity, the determination of the human author. In 1914 the Biblical Commission declared that the epistle must be considered canonical and also "among the genuine epistles of the Apostle Paul." The Commission added that it is not necessary to hold that "he [Paul] put it in exactly the form in which it now stands."

The mystery of Hebrews hinges on these questions: Who wrote it? To whom was it written, where and when? The reason for the questions is that the language, style, and thought differ so much from Paul's customary manner. At the same time there is much in Hebrews similar to ideas expressed in the other letters. Different answers are given to these questions. In a recent volume for the distinguished commentary *Études Bibliques*, Père Spicq has suggested Apollos as the author. Centuries ago Origen suggested Barnabas. These suggestions enjoy only probability at best. Nearly all Catholic exegetes agree that Paul is only the indirect author. They do not agree on the direct author. Non-Catholic critics for the most part date the epistle around A.D. 90, thus divorcing it from Paul.

There is also difference of opinion in regard to its destination. The title "to the Hebrews" is not original but a later inference drawn from the contents. Père Spicq proposes that it was written to a community of Jewish priests, converts from Judaism, residing probably at Antioch. He dates it before the destruction of the Temple, at about A.D. 67. The shadow of impending disaster already loomed over Jerusalem. It was written, he says, to console the discouraged converts tempted to return to their old religion. Therefore we find the emphasis on Christ the true high priest, and the unique sacrifice of Christ. Père Daniélou in his recent book, *The Dead Sea Scrolls and Primitive Christianity*, suggests that "it seems quite reasonable to view those to whom the Epistle was addressed as a group of Essenian priests" (p. 113). This is highly conjectural. Another stand entirely is taken by the majority of non-Catholic scholars, who propose that the epistle was addressed to Christians, not to converts from Judaism. Some Catholic scholars also prefer this interpretation (Dubarle, Wikenhauser).

It seems certain that the epistle is directed to a specific community that the author knows well (cf. 13:19), and which is threatened by a spiritual crisis (cf. 12:12). Without the customary epistolary introduction, the writer launches immediately into his theological statement with an array of Old Testament citations that establish the superiority of Christ and his revelation. The heart of the epistle is the section 4:14–10:18 in which the central Christological theme is developed, intermingled with frequent exhortation. It is this aspect that has led some to describe the epistle as a written sermon. The central theme is developed along these lines: Jesus is the true high priest (4:14–5:10), a perfect high priest forever according to the order of Melchisedech, superior to the levitical priesthood (7:1–28), high priest of the heavenly tabernacle, mediator of the New Testament which terminates the Old (8:1–13). Christ's atoning sacrifice is unique, perfect, and eternal (9:1–28). His sacrifice supersedes the inadequate sacrificial system of the old Law (10:1–18).

The seven remaining New Testament epistles are grouped together under the title "The Catholic Epistles." They are James, 1–2 Peter, 1–2–3 John, and Jude. The reason for the title "Catholic" is that for the most part they are intended for general circulation or for a wider circle of readers. The questions discussed pertained to the whole Church, or at least to large parts of it. With the exception of 2 and 3 John, which are proper letters, they fit the definition of epistles given above.

Five of these epistles are deuterocanonical—all save 1 John and 1 Peter. Together with Hebrews and Apocalypse they comprise the seven New Testament deuterocanonical books. They are termed deuterocanonical because their universal recognition as canonical came later than the other books, which are called protocanonical. As in the case of Hebrews we meet a fluctuation of opinion concerning these letters in the early centuries, different attitudes in the Eastern and Western churches. Gradually and progressively the doubts and questions disappeared. In several cases undoubtedly the doubts were due to the brevity of the letters. Of more serious character were the doubts cast on 2 Peter. These have been accentuated by modern criticism, and it is considered pseudonymous by independent critics and by some Catholic scholars.

The early reformers of the sixteenth century excluded some or all of the deuterocanonical books from the New Testament canon. The Calvinists did not take any positive stand against them, and later the other Reformed groups returned to the traditional position. Today there is no difference in Protestant and Catholic New Testament canons.

The first word of the last book of the New Testament in the original Greek is *apocalupsis*. It provides the title for the book in Catholic English versions, "The Apocalypse of St. John the Apostle." The word means "revelation," and this appears in the title in the Protestant versions; in the King James, "The Revelation of St. John the Divine"; in the Revised Standard, "The Revelation to John."

This book belongs to the genre termed apocalyptic which we met previously in discussing the book of Daniel. Apocalyptic passages occur in the earlier Old Testament prophets as well. There was a spate of apocalyptic writings during the centuries of late Judaism and early Christianity. Their one great theme is the final act of history, the end of this world and the coming of the other world. All this is depicted because of real or alleged revelations given by God.

The apocalypses have a language all their own. They speak in symbols, in numbers, in stars, and in beasts of various descriptions. The reader will recognize these features in the Apocalypse of John. He will observe the use of numbers. The frequently occurring number 7 is a symbol of perfection. When the Lamb is described as having seven horns and seven eyes the meaning is perfection of power, since the horn stands for power, and perfection of knowledge, since the eyes are a symbol of inner sight. The number 6 is the symbol of imperfection, and 666 makes one out to be in a very bad way. By a device known as gematria, numbers could conceal the name of a person. The number 666 conceals the name Caesar Nero, since the numerical equivalents of the Hebrew letters of the name come to the total 666. Note that the victor is depicted riding a white horse and his armies are robed in white. The color white is the symbol of victory. These examples will suffice to show that ideas and truths are expressed by symbols, and the symbols must be rightly understood before we can comprehend the meaning of the book. The interested reader is referred to *The Apocalypse of St. John* by H. M. Féret, o.p.

The true nature of the Apocalypse is overlooked by those

who would read into it the events of twentieth-century history or use it as a calendar to prophesy the end of the world. It is true that the meaning of the book is eschatological, but in the sense that it refers to the events of the end time, not in the sense that it dates it. It is not, however, purely eschatological. Its message was intended for primitive Christianity, and in figurative language it speaks of political and religious conditions contemporary with its first readers. Babylon for example is a symbolic name for pagan Rome. It follows that the eschatological meaning must be linked to its contemporary message. The former flows out of the historical meaning, for behind the struggle between Christian Church and the Roman Empire were aligned the heavenly and the infernal powers. The struggle between pagan Rome and Christianity was really a struggle between Satan and God, a rehearsal for that final great conflict between them when God's victory will mark the end of this world and the beginning of the other world. The Apocalypse is a Christian philosophy of history.

The question of the literary composition of the book is extremely complex. Most authors defend the unity of the work, but recently Fr. Boismard has proposed that the book is a conflation of two similar works written at different times. The arrangement of the text according to this theory may be seen in the Bible of Jerusalem. The earlier apocalypse would have been written before A.D. 70, the later one sometime after. The date assigned by tradition is the close of the reign of Domitian, about A.D. 95.

Tradition in the early Church was almost unanimous in the opinion that the author was John the Apostle, the most notable exception being Dionysius, bishop of Alexandria (+ 264). There were for a time doubts concerning the canonicity of the book, which caused it to be listed among the deuterocanonicals. The question of authorship is disputed because of the differences in style and thought between Apocalypse and the other writings of John the Apostle. Alfred Wichenhauser says, "If both are the work of the same author, there is really no satisfactory explanation of these divergencies" (*New Testament Introduction*, p. 553). Père Boismard suggests that it originated in the circle of John's followers and is a faithful expression of his teaching. Fr. Gaechter and others who defend the Johannine authorship ascribe the differences of style to a secretary who wrote down in Greek the Aramaic teaching of the Apostle. We have already noted that pseudonymous attribution was one of the characteristics of the apocalyptic genre.

The Apocalypse of John, despite its esoteric quality and the difficulty of its interpretation, has a very practical purpose: to console those who suffer persecution. It is for this reason that the book is so meaningful in our day. Its message of consolation is timeless, and its promise is the ultimate victory of good over evil, of Christ over Antichrist.

So the Scriptures, which open with the divine edict, "Let there be light" (Gen. 1:3), close with a human sigh, "Come, Lord Jesus!" (Apoc. 22:20). Maran-atha!

# APPENDICES

# THE SIGNIFICANCE OF QUMRAN

There have been occasional references in the preceding pages to the Dead Sea Scrolls. The reader may find it convenient to have here a brief statement on them and the community to which they are related. Their greatest interest to the average layman lies in their connection with Christian origins. That, too, we shall discuss.

## The Discovery

In 1947 a Bedouin shepherd accidentally came upon some leather scrolls in a cave near the gorge called Wady Qumran. The cliffs skirt the shores of the Dead Sea, and the scrolls were therefore described as the Dead Sea Scrolls. More accurately they are called the Qumran Scrolls. The site is located about seven miles south of Jericho. The discovery has been called by Prof. W. F. Albright of Johns Hopkins "the greatest manuscript discovery of modern times."

The discovery of 1947 was the beginning of a series of manuscript finds. Since that time eleven caves in the vicinity of Wady Qumran have given up manuscripts, the latest coming in January 1956 from Cave XI. The most important came from Caves I, IV, and XI. The total number of manuscripts from the Qumran area is more than five hundred, a few quite complete, the rest in fragments which run into tens of thousands.

The relatively intact manuscripts come from Caves I and XI. From Cave XI there are biblical and non-biblical documents. Among the biblical manuscripts are a well-preserved copy of the Psalms and one of Leviticus. The finds in Cave IV, although in bits and pieces, are perhaps the most important of all. About one-fourth of the total are biblical manuscripts that represent all the books of the Hebrew Bible with the exception of Esther. The others are works in the apocryphal and related genres, as well as a mass of sectarian literature. From Cave I came the seven scrolls that are most familiar to the layman, and which provided the basis for some early sensational interpretations. Among these was a copy of Isaias, practically complete; a commentary on the prophecy of Habacuc; and a document called at first the

Manual of Discipline, now referred to as the Rule of the Community. A fourth manuscript, opened only after some years of tedious effort, was first named the Apocalypse of Lamech; on being opened it proved to be an expansion of Genesis and is now called A Genesis Apocryphon. This lot of scrolls came into the possession of the Syrian Orthodox Archbishop of Jerusalem.

Three other scrolls from Cave 1 were purchased by Professor Sukenik of the Hebrew University in Jerusalem. This lot comprised a second incomplete scroll of Isaias, a collection of hymns, called the Thanksgiving Psalms, and a work of apocalyptic character called the Order of the War between the Children of Light and the Children of Darkness. All the scrolls from Cave 1 are now in possession of the Hebrew University. The scrolls of the Syrian Archbishop were purchased by the University in 1954 for the reported sum of $250,000. The transaction was made in the United States, where the scrolls had been brought by the Archbishop.

The scrolls are made available to the international community of scholars by publication. The published volumes reproduce the manuscripts in photographic plates accompanied by a transcription in Hebrew. The scrolls from Cave 1 have been published—those belonging to the Syrian Archbishop—by the American Schools of Oriental Research in 1950–51, with the exception of *A Genesis Apocryphon* which had a later preliminary publication. The scrolls originally acquired by the Hebrew University in Jerusa-

lem were published there in 1955. Assorted fragments from
Cave I have been published at Oxford in a volume entitled
*Discoveries in the Judaean Desert. 1.* It will be some years
before all the materials are published. An international
team of scholars of different religious confessions is engaged
in the tremendous task of identifying the fragments and
preparing them for publication. It is only upon publication
that the manuscripts become available to the average
scholar, and it is upon these fundamental publications that
he bases his research, whence come his articles of scientific
interpretation. Articles of a popular but reliable character
are published in the *Biblical Archeologist* of the American
Schools of Oriental Research.

For the sake of clarity we have not interrupted the discussion of the Qumran scrolls with a report on other discoveries
made in the same period. A brief note on them will suffice
here. There was a lull after 1947, but not for long. In 1951
the Bedouin had more scrolls for sale. They came, it was
learned, from caves about twelve miles southwest of
Qumran at Wady Murabba'at. Scientific excavations were
carried on there in 1952. The finds will be published in the
second volume of *Discoveries in the Judaean Desert.* The
manuscripts include letters from the time of the Second
Jewish Revolt (A.D. 132–135), a fine scroll of the Minor
Prophets from the second Christian century, and the
earliest Hebrew papyrus known from the seventh or eighth
century B.C. Still other manuscripts were found in 1952
at Khirbet Mird, site of ancient Hyrcania. The texts in-

cluded fragments of the book of Wisdom, the Gospels of Mark and John, and the Acts of the Apostles. They are written in Greek and date from the fifth to the eighth centuries A.D. There were Old Testament and New Testament fragments in the Syro-Palestinian language and script, as well as Arabic and Syriac papyri. Still other manuscripts come from a site known only to the Bedouin.

## The Excavations

The finds at Qumran stirred up many questions, particularly about the date of the scrolls and the people connected with them. In the hope of finding satisfactory answers to the questions, excavations were undertaken on the site of ruins near the caves, Khirbet Qumran. The diggings began in 1951 under the direction of Père de Vaux of the École Biblique and Lankester Harding of the Jordan Department of Antiquities. Five campaigns were conducted.

The excavations established the close connection of the occupants of the Qumran buildings with the scrolls found in caves. Jars identical with those of the caves were found. The community pottery works were identified. The scriptorium where scrolls were copied was uncovered; there were inkpots with dried remnants of ink. There were cisterns and an elaborate water supply system pointing to abundant use of water. There were large rooms, apparently assembly rooms. Coins were found by which the date of occupancy could be reliably established. The sum total of the archeological data revealed that the principal phase of occupancy ended in 68 B.C., the time of the first Jewish revolt against Rome. The result of the excavations was to confirm the early dating of the scrolls, namely, in the second and first pre-Christian centuries and the first Christian century. The second result was to confirm the opinion of those who had suggested that the Qumran community was related to the Essenes. In his recent and authoritative book, *The Ancient Library of Qumran and Modern Biblical Studies,* Prof. Frank M. Cross of Harvard declares that there is now sufficient evidence to identify the people of the scrolls with the Essenes "definitively."

Who were the Essenes? Prior to the discoveries at Qumran they were known chiefly from the works of the Jewish philosopher Philo (+ A.D. 50), the Jewish historian Flavius Josephus (+ c. A.D. 100), and the Roman Pliny the Elder (+ A.D. 79). They were described as one of the three orders of Judaism, along with the Pharisees and Sadducees, numbered about four thousand, and were represented in various cities. They were marked by strong separatist traits. Their followers practiced voluntary poverty, holding goods in common, and in general practiced celibacy. Characteristic features of their religious practices were ritualistic washings and sacred meals. Their religious beliefs included the idea of the immortality of the soul, belief in angels, and what Josephus describes as fatalism. Professor Cross contends that these sources are essentially confirmed by the Qumran scrolls, but must also be controlled by them. This control brings into better focus the apocalyptic character of the Essenes. Their roots are in the priestly laws of holiness of old Judaism and their outlook is toward the New Order that is soon to come, in which they will be the New Israel. In a word, the Qumran community may be described as a priestly apocalyptic sect.

## Significance

It will appear from what has been said that the Qumran non-biblical manuscripts provide us with primary source material on the Essenes. This is of the greatest importance to historians and to New Testament scholars for their investigation of New Testament backgrounds and the history of the primitive Church. This phase of research can be seen in the numerous articles in learned journals, or in books like Jean Daniélou's *The Dead Sea Scrolls and Primitive Christianity*. Resemblances have been shown to exist between the theological language of the scrolls and that of the New Testament, particularly in John and Paul. In comparing the Qumran sect with the primitive Christian community one notes immediately the community of goods in both and the emphasis on celibacy. Similarities in the organizational structure of the communities have also been noted. The large result of the comparative study is the relation of primitive Christianity and its writings to a Jewish milieu rather than to Hellenism. Professor Cross and others have emphasized the apocalyptic milieu common to Qumran and the early Church. We hardly need to say that these comparative studies point out the differences as well as the resemblances. The reader may rest assured that the originality of Christ and the Church has not been impaired.

The biblical scrolls from Qumran are of equal importance for Old Testament studies. This is seen quite dramatically in the Isaias scrolls from Cave 1. Prior to the discovery the oldest Hebrew witness to Isaias was a manuscript of the tenth century A.D. The Qumran Isaias is about a thousand years earlier. The biblical scrolls will serve scholars in reconstructing the history of the Old Testament text, in the critical evaluation of readings of the Masoretic text and the Septuagint, and in the study of Hebrew scripts. It is not too much to say that the scrolls have revolutionized the science of Old Testament textual criticism.

## The Controversy

The reader will observe that we have kept the discussion to fundamental and general lines. The reason was pedagogical method. General orientation must precede specific questions. We have not therefore asked such questions as these: Was John the Baptist an Essene? Was the Teacher of Righteousness named in the scrolls a Messias like Jesus? It was sensational answers to questions like these that gave rise to the controversy over the scrolls which we now describe.

We may date the beginning of this on May 26, 1950. On that day in Paris the "very original French orientalist" André Dupont-Sommer read a paper before the *Académie des Inscriptions et Belles Lettres*. With a flare for the dramatic, Dupont-Sommer presented his interpretation of the vague historical allusions in the *Habakkuk Commentary*. He created great astonishment by proposing that the Teacher of the scrolls was an exact prototype of Jesus, particularly as a martyred prophet. Now what happens at a French literary academy in Paris ordinarily has little repercussion on Americans. But in the course of events these ideas of Dupont-Sommer appeared in a book, which was soon translated into English. Still, a trim little volume in a staid English bookstore may escape general notice. It took something more to bring these ideas to Americans at large. They became aware of the sensational thesis of the very original French orientalist in 1955 when the May 14 issue of the *New Yorker* appeared on the stands. In a lengthy and gripping report titled "The Scrolls from the Dead Sea" Edmund Wilson projected the ideas of Dupont-Sommer on a large screen. Then America began to buzz with excitement about the Dead Sea Scrolls, the Essenes, the Teacher of Righteousness, the uniqueness of Jesus, and the originality of Christianity. Mr. Wilson's report later appeared in book form and soon took its place among the best-sellers, a position it held for months.

So that is the way it came about. Now what did the very original orientalist and the intrepid reporter have to say? That may best be answered by reading an excerpt from the Dupont-Sommer volume which was quoted by Mr. Wilson in his *New Yorker* article and later in his book. "Everything in the Jewish [i.e., the Qumran] New Covenant heralds and prepares the way for the Christian New Covenant. The Galilean Master as He is presented to us in the writings of the New Testament, appears in many respects as an astonishing reincarnation of the Teacher of Righteousness . . . . Like him, He was the elect and the Messiah of God, the Messiah Redeemer of the world. Like him, He was the object of the hostility of the priests, the party of the Sadducees. Like him, He was condemned and put to death . . . . Like him, at the end of time, He will be the supreme judge. Like him, He founded a Church whose adherents fervently awaited His glorious return" (A. Dupont-Sommer, *The Dead Sea Scrolls*, p. 99).

That is only a partial list, but it is enough to give you to understand why Christians were disturbed and confused. The fact that such a statement is without foundation in the scrolls is small comfort to the person who could read the *New Yorker* but could not read the scrolls. In a word, much unnecessary concern was caused on the part of many to whom Jesus means so much. The talents of intellectuals carry with them a social responsibility. It is regrettable that they sometimes forget this. I shall evaluate this sensational interpretation in a moment, but there are a few more details that I think the reader will find of interest.

In January of that year (1956) the New York *Times* correspondent in London reported on three broadcasts given by British professor John Marc Allegro on the B.B.C. Professor Allegro was quoted as saying that the wicked priest "dragged forth the Teacher [of Righteousness] as he himself was offering sacrifice at the altar, and, as now seems probable from a recently discovered manuscript, gave him into the hands of his Gentile mercenaries to be crucified." He concluded his broadcast with these words, "the scattered disciples [of the Teacher of Righteousness] returned and reverently buried the body of their Teacher in a tomb near by, where they settled down in a way of life he had ordained for them, to await his glorious return as Messiah of God"(The New York *Times*, January 24, 1956).

Do you blame the Christian listening to B.B.C. broadcasts—or readers of the New York *Times* report—for being disturbed and confused? What impression could they get but that the originality of the New Testament and the uniqueness of Jesus had gone up in smoke?

Now, what about all this? It goes without saying that it is sensational and that it makes news. It is also a known fact that retractions and denials are not as sensational and as newsworthy as these first melodramatic headlines. In any case, let us see first the reaction to Professor Allegro's broadcasts. The remarks of the young professor had assumed a particular prestige because he was part of the team of scholars working on the scrolls. After the broadcasts five of his colleagues, scholars also working on the scrolls, wrote this letter to the London *Times:* "In view of the broad repercussions of [Allegro's] statement, and the fact that the materials on which they are based are not yet available to the public, we, his colleagues, feel obliged to make the following statement: There are no unpublished texts at the disposal of Mr.

Allegro other than those of which the originals are at present in the Palestine Archeological Museum where we are working. Upon the appearance in the press of citations from Mr. Allegro's broadcasts we have reviewed all the pertinent materials, published and unpublished. We are unable to see in the text the 'findings' of Mr. Allegro. We find no crucifixion of the 'teacher,' . . . no 'broken body of their Master' to be stood guard over until Judgment Day . . . . It is our conviction that either he had misread the texts or he has built up a chain of conjectures which the materials do not support" (*Time*, April 2, 1956). The young professor received a more severe castigation from his former teacher, Professor Rowley of Manchester University. Professor Rowley said, "I deplore as unscholarly the presentation to the world of what scholars everywhere have supposed —as I supposed—to be specific statements in an unpublished text to which Mr. Allegro alone had access, when they are only deductions from evidence which is capable of other interpretations . . . . Important documents . . . should not be used to give immature scholars a spurious authority" (*Ibid.*).

Let us return now to M. Dupont-Sommer. When his daring thesis became known there was a great reaction of opposition from the scholarly world, and great debate ensued. A few years later, in 1953, the very original orientalist wrote a second book about the scrolls. In this book his views were greatly modified and much more moderate. Since the situation was, to say the least, by this time more than a little confused, *The Saturday Review* wrote to M. Dupont-Sommer to this effect: "Since it is generally believed that your second book is more cautious than is your first book *The Saturday Review* would like to know whether you . . . continue to believe that there is evidence in the scrolls which may deny the uniqueness and the divinity of Jesus. Do you find any new evidence for believing that orthodox Christian thinking may have to be revised in the light of the Dead Sea Scrolls?"

Here is the answer of the French scholar as reported in *The Saturday Review:* "I never claimed that the Dead Sea Scrolls could strike a blow against the 'uniqueness' of Jesus . . . . I believe that the Dead Sea Scrolls do not deny the divinity of Jesus [even] in the sense of 'Son of God Incarnate.' In a general sense, viewed as a whole, the originality of the Christian Church seems to me to remain unchanged" (*The Saturday Review*, March 3, 1956). I am tempted to say at this point, "After the tempest comes the small still voice," or rather to ask, "Was this tempest necessary?"

This controversy has been described by a recent writer as "the most inglorious chapter of the communication of the finds of the desert of Juda to the general public."[1] Theologians and biblical scholars are able to take these extravagant interpretations in stride and evaluate them critically. The same cannot be said for the general reader. As a result the

[1] J. Van der Ploeg, *The Excavations at Qumran* (Longmans, 1958), p. 189.

issue becomes confused in the public mind and doubts and uncertainties prevail. The controversy is now laid to rest in scholarly circles, but its ghost may haunt us for a while. In good time the ghost, too, will be laid by that sober and devoted scholarship which serves man best.

## NOTES ON THE CHART

The chart is designed to serve as a supplement to Chapter Three. The books of the Bible are placed in the periods of history in which the events they record took place, though in their present form they may date from a later period. Thus, the events recorded in Deuteronomy took place in the thirteenth century B.C., whereas the book as we know it belongs to the seventh century.

The titles of some books of the Bible differ in Catholic and Protestant editions. These also differ frequently in the spelling of names. Where there is a notable difference, the corresponding title or the Protestant edition is indicated in parenthesis; e.g., Abdias (Obadiah). Certain books of the Old Testament named on the chart are not found in Protestant editions for reasons explained in Chapter Two.

| | ANCIENT NEAR EAST | | | BOOKS OF THE BIBLE | | |
| | EGYPT | MESOPOTAMIA, etc. | PALESTINE | HISTORICAL | PROPHETIC | DIDACTIC |
| --- | --- | --- | --- | --- | --- | --- |
| B.C. 2000-1500 | The Middle Kingdom 2000-1780<br><br>Hyksos Domination c.1700-1570<br><br>The New Kingdom c.1546 | The Amorite Invasions 2000-1700 (The Mari Age)<br><br>Babylonian Empire (Hammurabi c.1700)<br><br>Irruption of Highland Peoples (Kassites) | Under Egyptian control for most of this period<br><br>c.1850 Hebrew Patriarchs Israel in Egypt | Genesis 1-11: Pre-history Genesis 12-50 | | |
| B.C. 1500-1200 | Imperial Expansion under Thutmose III c.1500-1450<br><br>Religious Revolt of Amenophis IV (Akhenaton) c.1365-<br><br>(el-Amarna Letters) | Babylonia weak under Kassite rule<br><br>Mitanni or Hurrian Kingdom c.1500-1370<br><br>Hittite Empire in Asia Minor 1600-1200 | Province of Egypt<br><br>Conquest by Israel after Exodus and Desert Wandering c.1225 | Exodus Deuteronomy Numbers Leviticus<br>Josue | | |
| B.C. 1200-1000 | Invasion of Sea Peoples (Philistines) c.1190<br><br>Decline of Power | No powerful rulers: except Tiglath-Pileser I c.1114-1076 | Invasion of Philistines c.1190<br><br>Period of Judges in Israel<br><br>Beginning of Israelite Monarchy c.1040 | Judges. Ruth<br><br>1 Samuel | | |

| Period | Egypt | Empire | History | 2 Samuel | Israel | Juda | Writings |
|---|---|---|---|---|---|---|---|
| B.C. 1000-539 | Egypt weak under Libyan and Ethiopian Dynasties | Assyrian Empire 1000-612<br><br>Chaldean Empire (Neo-Babylonian) 612-539 | United Monarchy under David and Solomon 1010-931<br>Divided Monarchy 931-931<br>Fall of Samaria 722<br><br>Fall of Jerusalem 586<br>Babylonian Captivity | 2 Samuel<br>1-2 Paralipomenon (Chronicles)<br>3 Kings (1 Kings)<br><br>4 Kings (2 Kings)<br>Tobias | Amos<br>Osee | Micheas (Micah)<br>Isaias 1-35<br>Sophonias<br>Nahum<br>Habacuc<br>Jeremias<br>Ezechiel<br>Isaias 40-55<br>Lamentations<br>Baruch | Psalms<br>Proverbs<br>- - - - - - -<br>- - - - - - -<br>Job ↓<br>Canticle ↓ |
| B.C. 539-333 | Conquered by Cambyses of Persia 525 | Persian Empire 539-333 | Return from Exile c.538<br><br>Esdras 458<br>Nehemias 445-433 | Esdras<br>Nehemias. Judith<br>Esther | | Aggeus (Haggai)<br>Zacharias<br>Isaias 56-66<br>Malachias<br>Joel<br>Abdias (Obadiah)<br>Jonas | |
| B.C. 333-63 | Subject to Alexander and to Ptolemies | Period of Hellenism 333-63 | Subject to Ptolemies to 198<br>then to Seleucids<br>Revolt of Machabees | 1-2 Machabees | | Daniel | Ecclesiastes<br>Wisdom<br>Sirach |
| B.C. 63-A.D. 325 | Subject to Rome | Roman Empire 63 B.C.—325 A.D. | Herod the Great 37-4 B.C.<br>Pontius Pilate 26-36 A.D.<br>Destruction of Jerusalem 70 A.D. | Mark<br>Matthew<br>Luke<br>John | Apocalypse (Revelation) | | Epistles of St. Paul<br>Catholic Epistles |

## BASIC READING PLAN

### THE OLD TESTAMENT

| | |
|---|---|
| Genesis | The origin of the human family; the advent of sin; the origin of the tribes of Israel.<br><br>*Theological Significance:* God calls Abraham from paganism, promises him a great nation and the land of Canaan, and promises that in him all nations of the earth shall be blessed. |
| Exodus<br>Numbers<br>Josue<br>Judges<br>Ruth | The Lord (Yahweh) elects Israel as his own people, manifests his power in Egypt, gives the Law at Sinai; Israel becomes the covenanted people of the Lord.<br><br>*Theological Significance:* Israel's destiny in history is bound up with the worship of Yahweh alone and fidelity to the Covenant-Law. |
| 1. 2 Samuel<br>3. 4 Kings<br>(1.2 Kings)<br>Amos<br>Osee<br>Isaias 1–35<br>Jeremias<br>Lamentations<br>Ezechiel<br>Isaias 40–55 | The Lord makes a covenant with the dynasty of David and promises it perpetuity. Jerusalem capital of a united Israel. The Temple of Solomon the heart of worship in Israel. The division of the kingdom. Downfall of the northern kingdom because of infidelity and idolatry. Jerusalem and Temple destroyed. Juda in exile.<br><br>*Theological Significance:* The Messianic hope was bound up with the dynasty of David. Despite the national disaster Messianic hope survives in the remnant of the people as foretold by the prophets. |

| | |
|---|---|
| *Esdras*<br>*Nehemias*<br>*Aggeus*<br>*Zacharias*<br>*Isaias* 56–66 | The remnant returns. The second common-wealth is established. The Second Temple is built. The covenant is renewed. This is the period of Jews and Judaism.<br><br>*Theological Significance:* Spiritually puri-fied by the experience of the exile, Juda takes on the character of a religious state. The religion of Judaism develops around the Torah and the Temple. |
| 1 *Machabees*<br>*Daniel* | The Jews revolt against Syrian persecution and win independence.<br><br>*Theological Significance:* The expectancy of the Messias grows more intense. |
| *Psalms* | On theme of creation<br>    8.18.28.32.102.103.138<br>On themes of Israelite history<br>    80.94.104.113.134.136.146<br>On Jerusalem and the Temple<br>    41.42.83.121<br>On themes of royalty and the Messias<br>    2.21.44.88.109.131<br>On wisdom<br>    14.22.23.33.48.50.61.111.127.132 |
| *Job*<br>*Proverbs*<br>*Wisdom*<br>*Canticle* | On wisdom and love and faith |

## THE NEW TESTAMENT

*Mark*
*Matthew*
*Luke*
*John*
*1. 2. 3 John*

> Jesus is the fulfillment of the Messianic hope of the Old Testament. He is the divine Messias.

*Acts*
*1. 2 Thessalonians*
*Galatians*
*Romans*
*1. 2 Corinthians*
*Philippians*
*Ephesians*
*Colossians*
    or
*Philemon*
*1. 2 Timothy*
*Titus*
*Hebrews*
*James*
*1. 2 Peter*
*Jude*

> The Church established by Christ is the kingdom of God on earth. It is the new order, the New Covenant, that replaces the old and fulfills the promise made to Abraham.

*Apocalypse*

> The Christian philosophy of history expressed in apocalyptic imagery: the conflict between the City of God and the City of Man until the ultimate victory of Jesus at his Second Coming and the glorious consummation of his kingdom in heaven.